17 JAN 2013

KID MADE MODERN

TODD OLDHAM

AMMO

TABLE OF CONTENTS

WHAT IS MODERN?

Welcome to
KID MADE MODERN!
This book is like three books in one.
It is full of fun, stimulating, easy-to-follow
projects—52 to be exact. It also celebrates
some of the most interesting designers and artists
from around the world. KID MADE MODERN honors and
loves the talented group of women and men who were
part of the Modernist design movement. They believed
that good and exciting design was for everyone.
That's certainly a modern idea! The *ALL ABOUT* pages explain
the basics of art materials and techniques. These ideas and
suggestions are just a tiny part of the world of art and design.
You will learn and invent new ways to express yourself!
The projects in this book are inspired by modern design ideas
from the 1930s to 1960s—quite a long time ago.
WHAT IS MODERN? Is it the very newest idea or could it
be an old idea that still feels new? I think that it is
often both. Some of the projects in this book
require adult assistance so be sure to ask
for help when it's needed. Always
remember, SAFETY FIRST!

Good luck and
go make art,
toddoldham

ALL ABOUT
SUPPLIES

A well-stocked craft supply kit is a treasure. Think of it as a giant box of possibilities. Here is a list of most of the supplies we used in making the projects for the book.

BOBBI PINS

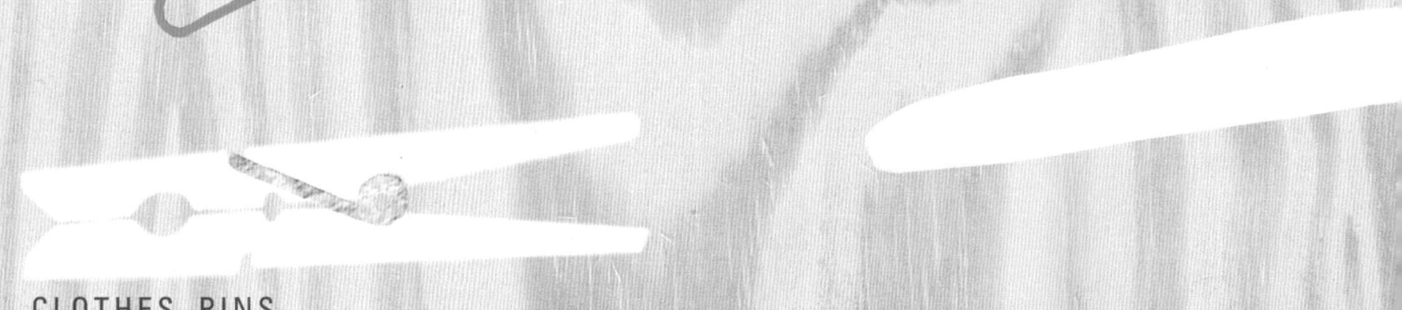

CLOTHES-PINS

MARKERS

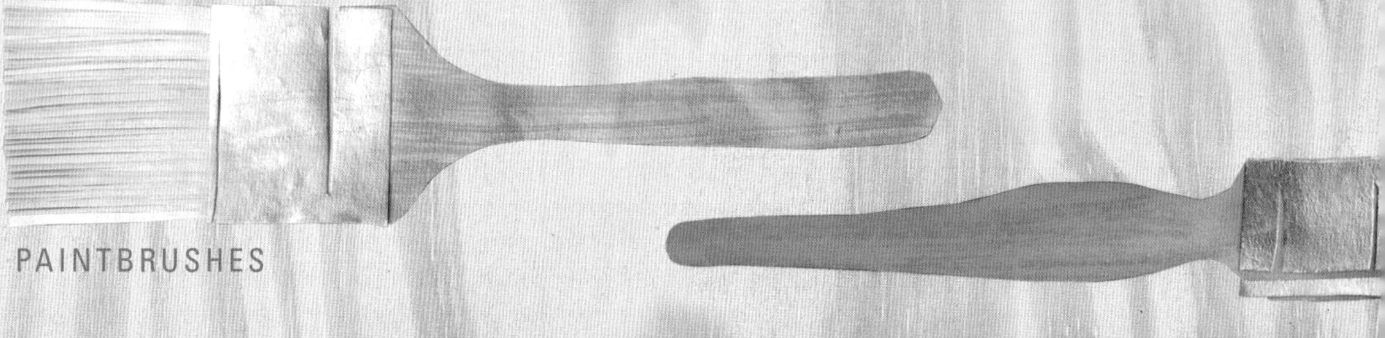

PAINTBRUSHES

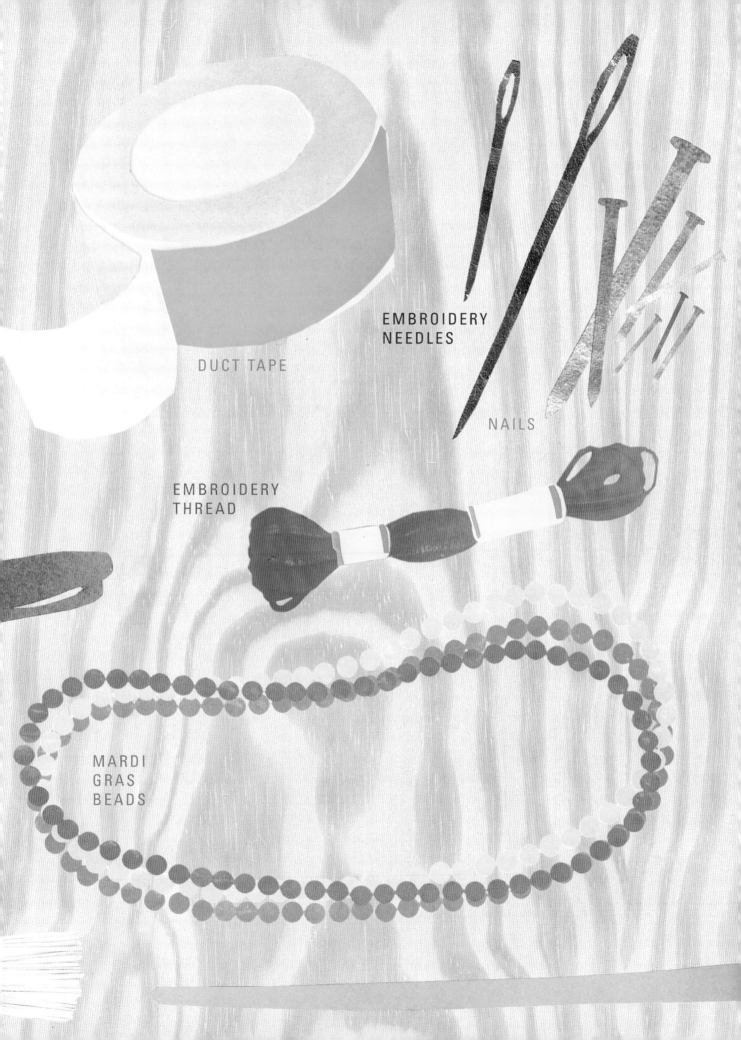

DUCT TAPE

EMBROIDERY
NEEDLES

NAILS

EMBROIDERY
THREAD

MARDI
GRAS
BEADS

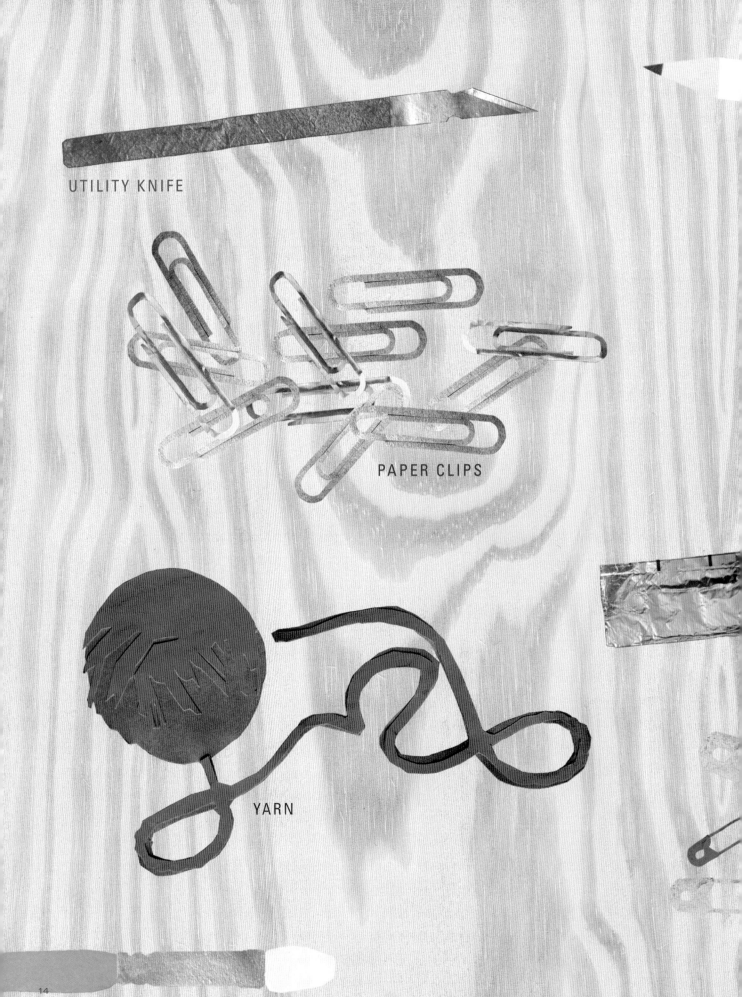

UTILITY KNIFE

PAPER CLIPS

YARN

PENCIL

PAINT

PAINT

CELLOPHANE TAPE

RULER

MORE
SUPPLIES
----
canvas
craft foam
dry dye
felt
glue stick
hammer
hole punch
Mod Podge
paper
push pins
scissors
tape measure
textile paint
thread

TWINE

SAFETY PINS

Paint comes in loads of colors and varieties. While all paint is pigment—a powder of pure color, mixed with a binder that holds it together—they all are very different. It is important to try all kinds of paints to find which ones you like working with.

ALL ABOUT
PA

OIL paint is a very slow drying paint that has been used for over 700 years. Oil paint is pure color pigment mixed in an oil base like linseed oil. It can be made opaque or transparent by thinning down the paint. Thin the paint or clean the brushes with turpentine or mineral spirits. Oil paint cannot be mixed with water. Oil paints are long lasting and stand the test of time. Due to flammable thinners, oil paints are best used by adults.

TEMPERA is a water-based paint that is like acrylic but the pigment is mixed with a variety of water-based binders like honey, milk or eggs. It has been used for thousands of years and is long lasting and dries quickly. Today it is either used in fine arts or in a lower quality for painting posters.

WATERCOL

OIL

TEMPERA

WATERCOLOR is the oldest kind of paint. The ancient cave paintings were made with watercolors of a sort. Watercolor paint is really just pigment mixed in a water-soluble medium. Watercolors can be very transparent and can be layered to come up with different colors. Watercolors travel easily and are used for painting on location. And it is the easiest to cleanup!

ACRYLIC paint is fast-drying paint containing pigment mixed in a plastic like fluid. Acrylic paints can be diluted with water yet once dry they are resistant to water. Heavily diluted acrylic can resemble watercolor while undiluted it can look like oil paint. Latex house paint is a kind of acrylic. Acrylic is less smelly than oil paint and easier to clean up.

GOUACHE is like the cousin to watercolors as it is made in the same way, almost. Gouache has larger pigment flakes as well as chalk that adds opacity. Gouache is more reflective, which means the colors seem brighter but are more difficult to layer. It is best used on paper or illustration board or even gessoed wood panels

ALL ABOUT
COLOR MIXING

Color mixing is one of the best magic tricks there is. If you know a little about the science of color mixing you will end up with happy results instead of only lovely shades of mud.

There are three basic colors from which other colors are made. They are called *primary* colors — red, blue and yellow. You cannot mix other colors to come up with these.

When you mix two primaries together you get a *secondary* color. When you mix three primary colors together or one primary and one secondary you get a *tertiary* color. Not all colors are mixed evenly; sometimes a lot of one color and just a little of another is all you need for the perfect shade. With a little experimentation you can come up with great colors that may even surprise you.

Black and white are like primary colors in that they cannot be made by mixing other colors together. You can mix your colors with white to lighten them or black to darken them. Some painters don't use black at all because it can overpower other colors. You can darken colors using other colors than black, like navy or brown.

The rules of color mixing do work and different types of paints mix differently, so it is always good to mix a small test amount before you mix a lot of one color to make sure you are getting what you want.

The tone of the colors you are mixing will affect the mixed colors. Red mixed with blue makes purple, and to be specific, navy blue and dark red make a deep purple shade while cherry red and cobalt blue make a bright grape color.

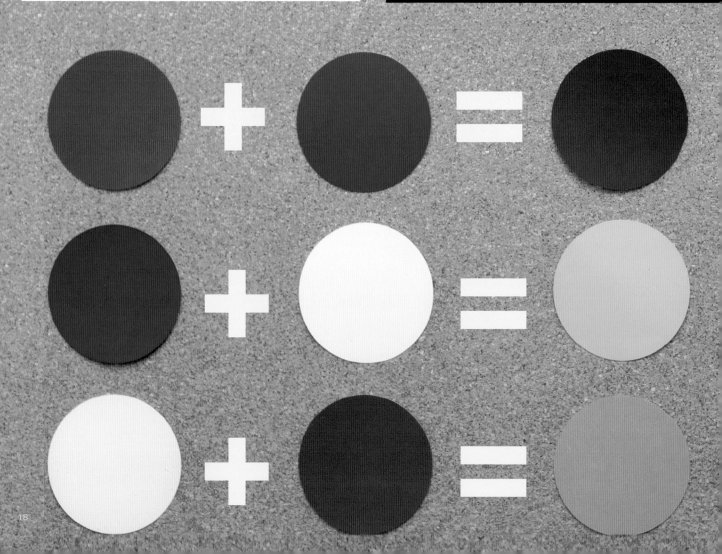

18

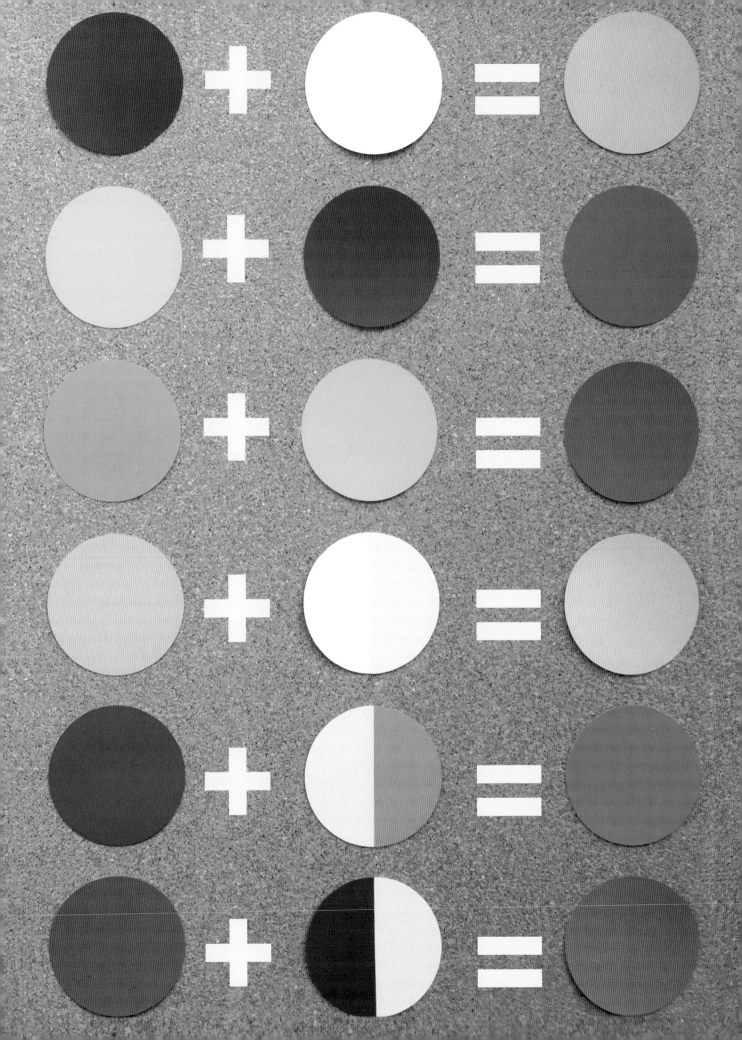

ALL ABOUT
COLOR
BLENDING

Color blending is the gradual transition of one color to another. Blending in white is used when making a tone lighter and black is used when making a tone darker, a technique used in painting to express shadow and light. Blending two different colors together can create unusual new colors between them. Notice the murky grayish blues between purple and indigo and the bright lime greens between yellow and green. Feel free to play with blending paint often. The more you know about how it works, the easier it is to express your ideas.

ROUND WATERCOLOR

SPONGE

STENCIL

FILBERT

ALL PURPOSE

ALL ABOUT

MOP

ROUND OIL

TOOTHBRUSH

FAN

FLAT

LOEW-CORNELL 322 FAN CHINA

XL Loew-Co

BRUSHES come in many sizes and materials. Their bristles can be made of synthetic fibers, plant fibers or animal hairs. Learning to use the right brush for your project will help make creating your artwork easier. Always clean your brushes well after each use and store them bristle end up. Most brushes will last a very long time if you take good care of them. Happy painting!

BRUSHES

ROUND WATERCOLOR brushes are simliar to the round oil brushes but work best with watercolors.

SPONGE brushes are best used on smooth surfaces. This brush leaves no stroke marks and is good for applying water-based paints and stains. This brush is affordable and disposable.

STENCIL brushes have a flat top bristle head which works well for pushing paint through stencil cut-outs.

FILBERT brushes have a flattened oval head and are used with oil and acrylic paint. It can be made from natural bristles, sable or cruelty-free synthetic fibers.

ALL PURPOSE brushes are affordable and used for many purposes. They are not meant to last a long time and finding a few stray bristles that have fallen out is normal.

MOP brushes are able to hold a large amount of fluid paint. It is soft and mop like, best used with watercolors or gouache.

ROUND OIL brushes come in many sizes. The round shape allows them to hold a great deal of paint. You may paint thin lines by painting with light pressure or paint thicker ones by pressing down firmly.

TOOTHBRUSHES can create a speckle and spray effect. Fill the toothbrush bristles with water-based paint and use your thumb to pull back the bristles and flick the paint onto paper.

FAN brushes have a thin layer of bristles that spread out like a fan. It is a super tool to blend colors or for creating feathery textures.

FLAT brushes are thin and wide and are available in many sizes. The bristles can be short for precise painting or longer for looser strokes that hold more paint. Works well with oil or water-based paint.

ALEXANDE

Alexander Girard made it look not very hard to make great fabric designs using crisp shapes and lines.

GIRARD

He was talented and brave;
he could design it all,

from airplanes to teacups,

he even made dolls!

SPOON FRIENDS

These fun to paint wooden spoon friends were inspired by Alexander Girard's beautiful wooden dolls that he handmade for his family in 1963.

SUPPLIES

YOU WILL NEED
unfinished wooden spoons,
shoe box,
acrylic paints,
brushes,
painter's tape,
paper plates,
pencil,
utility knife,
ruler

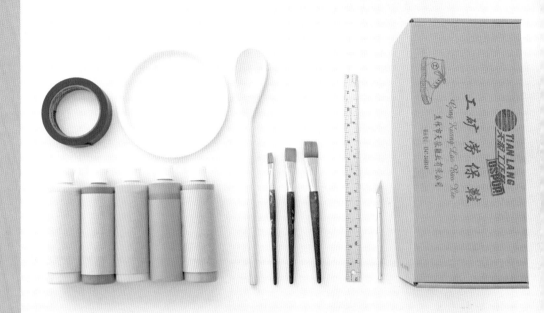

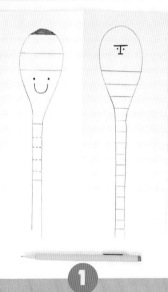

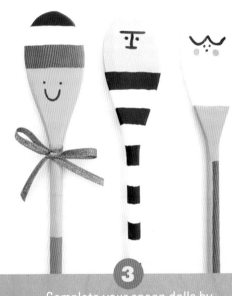

1

ce a wooden spoon on scrap paper.
stripes and facial expressions to your
awing. Use this as your template.

2

Working from the top down, mask off
your stripes with painter's tape, and
paint. Let dry and remove tape.

3

Complete your spoon dolls by
painting a face on each and
maybe add a bow tie too.

4

ake a display for your dolls out of a
e box painted in your favorite colors.

5

Ask an adult to cut Xs with a sharp
knife where you want your dolls to stand.

6

After playing with a spoon friend
push its handles through the X.

BLOCK PARTY

Build your own world with these brightly painted wooden blocks celebrating the shapes and colors of Alexander Girard.

YOU WILL NEED
wood scraps, non-toxic acrylic paint,
non-toxic water-based polyurethane,
paint brushes, painter's tape, pencil

Ask an adult to cut and sand smooth different sizes of wooden blocks. Wipe off all dust with a moist cloth, making sure there are no rough edges. With a pencil, sketch the shapes you wish to paint and mask them off with painter's tape.

1

2

Paint the exposed areas of the blocks using thin layers of paint. Let dry and remove the tape.

Re-tape over the previously painted areas and paint the next color. When you are finished painting, ask an adult to spray a non-toxic water-based polyurethane to protect the wood and paint.

THESE BLOCKS ARE NOT RECOMMENDED FOR CHILDREN UNDER 4 YEARS OLD.

3

STYLISH STAMPING

Stamp
sharp geometric
shapes like Alexand[er]
Girard, or create yo[ur]
very own! Custom fabr[ic]
and T-shirt designs ar[e]
simple to make, just use[e]
makeup sponges and
textile paint.

YOU WILL NEED
100% cotton T-shirt, makeup sponges, paper plates,
fabric paints, cardboard, white glue, aluminum foil

1

To make the stamp, cut a rectangle of cardboard
and glue the makeup sponge down in the middle.

2

You can cut the sponges into any shape
you like. This stamp looks like a bow tie.

3

Pour a little of your fabric paint onto a paper
plate. Use scrap cardboard to smear an even
layer of paint all the way to the edge of the plate.

4

Place your stamp into the paint and press down
lightly to make sure your sponge is covered evenly.

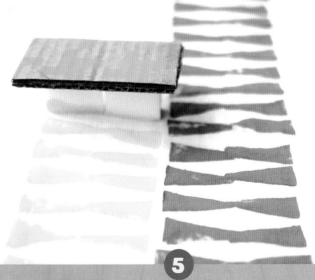

5

Place foil inside the shirt to avoid the paint soaking through and
start stamping! Let dry, following the paint's setting instructions.

STRIPE DREAMS

Alexander Girard loves bold playful stripes and so can you! Make your very own striped headboard using duct tape and gator board. Bedtime will be very restful, full of sweet colorful dreams.

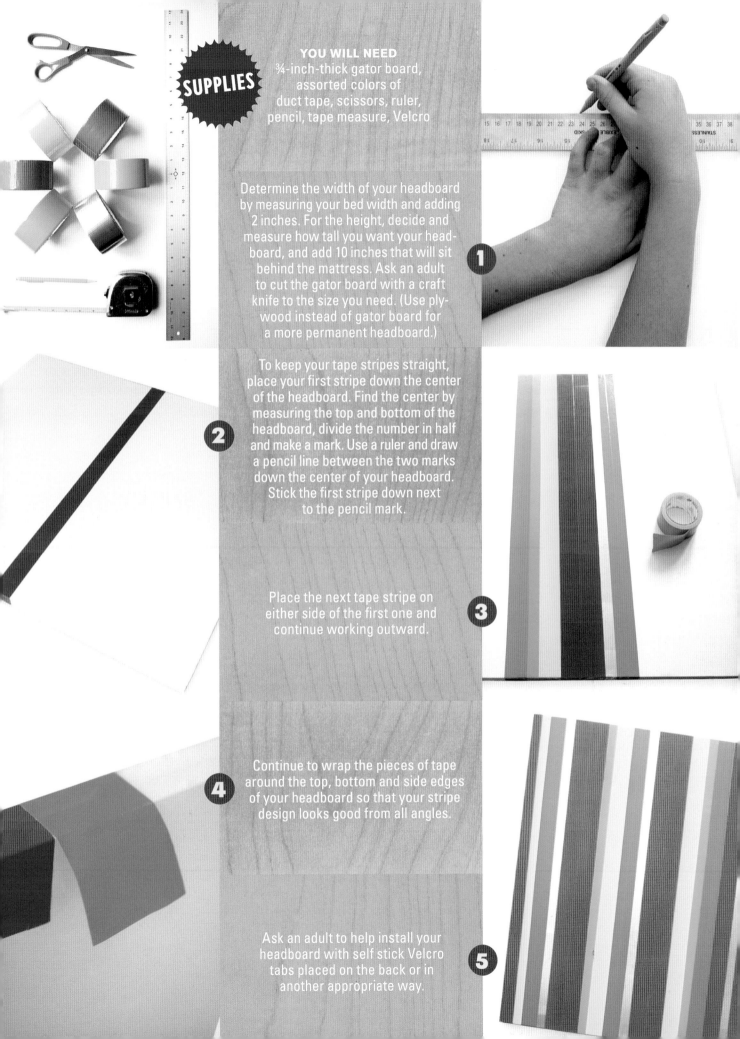

SUPPLIES

YOU WILL NEED
¾-inch-thick gator board,
assorted colors of
duct tape, scissors, ruler,
pencil, tape measure, Velcro

1 Determine the width of your headboard by measuring your bed width and adding 2 inches. For the height, decide and measure how tall you want your headboard, and add 10 inches that will sit behind the mattress. Ask an adult to cut the gator board with a craft knife to the size you need. (Use plywood instead of gator board for a more permanent headboard.)

2 To keep your tape stripes straight, place your first stripe down the center of the headboard. Find the center by measuring the top and bottom of the headboard, divide the number in half and make a mark. Use a ruler and draw a pencil line between the two marks down the center of your headboard. Stick the first stripe down next to the pencil mark.

3 Place the next tape stripe on either side of the first one and continue working outward.

4 Continue to wrap the pieces of tape around the top, bottom and side edges of your headboard so that your stripe design looks good from all angles.

5 Ask an adult to help install your headboard with self stick Velcro tabs placed on the back or in another appropriate way.

DUCT tape is sturdy, very sticky vinyl reinforced fabric tape that is used for temporary household repairs. It comes in a rainbow of colors, most commonly in silver, and is perfect for lots of crafts. It can be found in the hardware section of stores.

DUCT

CELLOPHANE tape is a transparent tape that when applied seems to disappear. It is often used when wrapping presents. It can come with one side or two sides being sticky and in shiny or frosted finishes. It is also manufactured with a double-sided light adhesive and called removable poster tape, perfect for hanging temporary artworks on walls.

CELLOPHANE

ALL ABOUT

TA

TAPE comes in rolls of many sizes and lengths. There are lots of different kinds of tape made for every kind of usage. Make sure to use the right tape for the right project and you always have success.

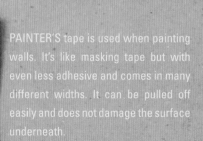

PAINTER'S

PAINTER'S tape is used when painting walls. It's like masking tape but with even less adhesive and comes in many different widths. It can be pulled off easily and does not damage the surface underneath.

MASKING tape is often found in an artist's studio and kitchen drawers. It's an all-purpose tape that was invented for masking off details when new cars were painted. This tape has less adhesive so it removes easily and won't damage the surface it was stuck to.

ARTIST'S tape is popular with artists, who use it to hold artwork in position in a frame. It is acid free and pH neutral, which means the chemicals in the adhesive will not stain artwork over time.

ELECTRICAL

ELECTRICAL tape is a ¾ inch tape used by electricians to wrap around wires that conduct electricity. It is made of plastic or vinyl and comes in different colors to identify the voltage of the wire.

CORK JUG

Masking tape can fake you out in this super-fast project. Roughly torn masking tape and shoe polish are all you need to turn anything into cork!

YOU WILL NEED
recycled bottle, masking tape,
brown shoe polish, paper towels

BROWN SHOE POLISH

1 Clean the bottle well and dry. Wrap a 6 inch length of masking tape around the bottle opening. Tear tape into approximately 1 inch-long pieces and stick them to the bottle overlapping and smoothing the edges. Start at the bottleneck and work down until the entire bottle is covered.

2 Make sure all tape edges are flat. Dab a cloth rag into brown shoe polish and rub it lightly over the entire bottle making sure to cover all the tape. Shoe polish sometimes has a strong smell so work in an open space.

3 Use a clean paper towel to wipe off any excess polish. Press down any loose ends of tape and let the bottle dry overnight. Fill your jug carefully with water; it's best not to get the tape wet. Put flowers into your jug and enjoy!

VASE LINES

Electrify any surface with different colors of plastic electrical tape. Just start by sticking it down and wrapping it around. Then trim off the rest.

SUPPLIES

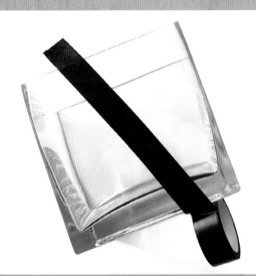

1 Clean the vase well and dry. Starting at the bottom of the vase, stick and wrap one color of electrical tape all the way around the vase.

Repeat, wrapping the tape stripes in other colors of electrical tape until the vase is about half covered or whenever you decide you have enough stripes.

2

3 Ask an adult to carefully trim off the excess tape with a utility knife right at the vase's edge and smooth down any loose edges of tape. Electrical tape is waterproof but the adhesive is not, so it's best not to get the tape wet.

Designer Verner Panton was actually quite groovy,
He made furniture that could have come from a science fiction movie.

He mixed new materials like plastics, foil and chrome into wild environments that some people called home.

POM
POM
RUG
RUG

Make a cozy rug from a plush pile of pom poms in colors inspired by Verner Panton. You will need 15 pom poms to create the triangle shaped rug that Ann is modeling right here. Try designing your own shapes and colors, and make one that is just for yo

YOU WILL NEED
3 colors of yarn, rubber grip liner (for kitchen cabinets), ruler, scissors, embroidery needle

SUPPLIES

Cut 2 cardboard discs 6½" across with a 1 inch hole in the center. Use a protractor or a bowl or plate around 6½" across, and trace around it to make a perfect circle.

1 Place the discs together. Wind 4 foot long pieces of yarn, starting at the center hole and wrapping around the outside edge and back through the middle hole over and over. Alternate colors of yarn as you work around the disc until the discs are covered.

2 Wiggle a pair of scissors between the two cardboard discs and cut through the loop all the way around. Tie a single piece of yarn in a knot around the bunch of yarn right at the center hole of the discs.

3 Gently wiggle the yarn out of the discs. Tie another piece of yarn around your first one for reinforcement. Fluff up yarns to make a ball, and trim off any long yarn.

4 Cut an 18 inch by 24 inch rectangle out of the rubber grip liner. Stitch through the liner, through the center of the pom pom, and then back through the liner. Tie a secure knot.

5 Stitch the pom poms to the liner in rows, 5 at the bottom, 4 centered on the next line above, then 3, then 2, then 1, forming a triangle shape. Trim off the excess rubber grip liner and yarn knots to 1 inch long.

TAPE TOTE

Like many of Verner Panton's designs, this bag is both space age and sturdy. We made this messenger bag using only duct tape and an envelope. You can use the same techniques and make a wallet or a tote too!

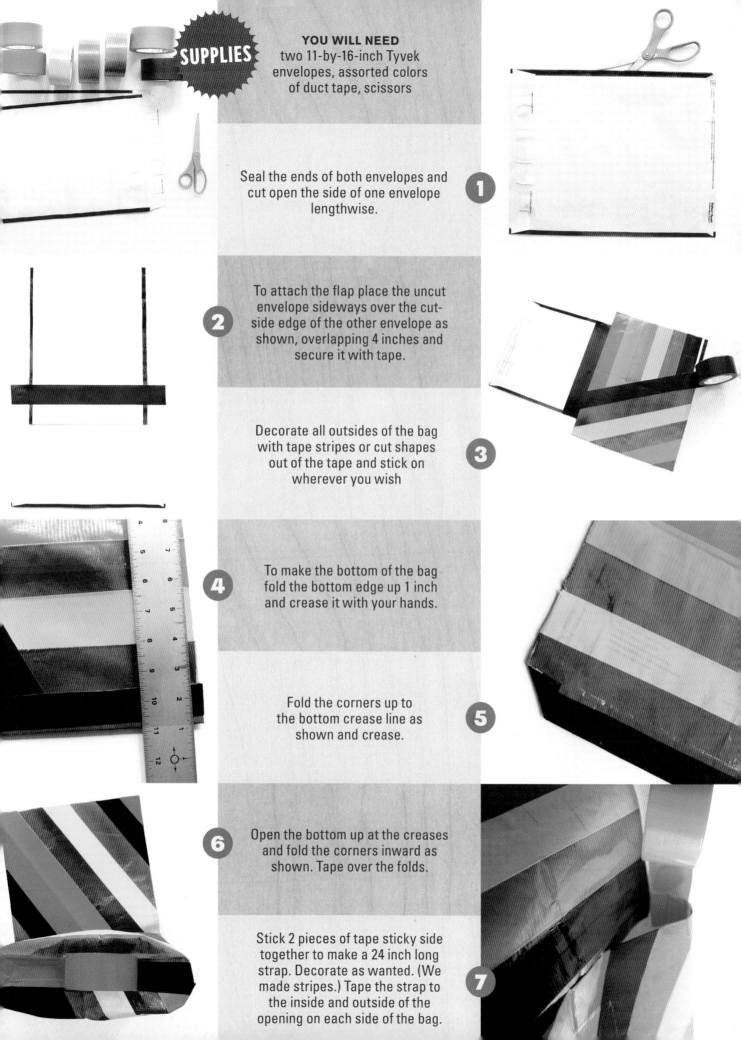

YOU WILL NEED
two 11-by-16-inch Tyvek
envelopes, assorted colors
of duct tape, scissors

1 Seal the ends of both envelopes and cut open the side of one envelope lengthwise.

2 To attach the flap place the uncut envelope sideways over the cut-side edge of the other envelope as shown, overlapping 4 inches and secure it with tape.

3 Decorate all outsides of the bag with tape stripes or cut shapes out of the tape and stick on wherever you wish

4 To make the bottom of the bag fold the bottom edge up 1 inch and crease it with your hands.

5 Fold the corners up to the bottom crease line as shown and crease.

6 Open the bottom up at the creases and fold the corners inward as shown. Tape over the folds.

7 Stick 2 pieces of tape sticky side together to make a 24 inch long strap. Decorate as wanted. (We made stripes.) Tape the strap to the inside and outside of the opening on each side of the bag.

COOL CUFFS

Recycle clear plastic bottles into custom cuffs of your very own design. Just draw your own patterns using permanent markers on fabric, roll out the bottle and glue it down!

YOU WILL NEED
clear plastic bottle with smooth surface
areas, cloth, permanent markers, tacky glue,
duct tape, cardboard, scissors

1

Very carefully cut just the smooth section
out of the middle of the plastic bottle.

2

Cut down the side of the plastic tube.

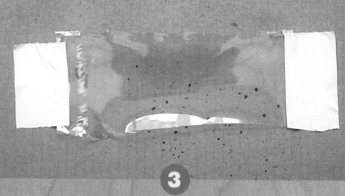

3

Roll out the plastic and duct-tape it down
to the cardboard with the "curling" side up.

4

Apply a thin even layer of tacky glue to the plastic.

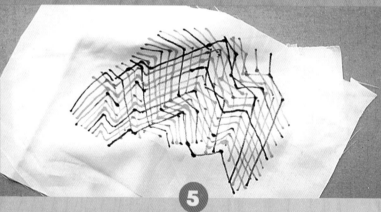

5

Draw designs on the fabric with markers. Place fabric
face-down onto the glue, pat down and let dry.

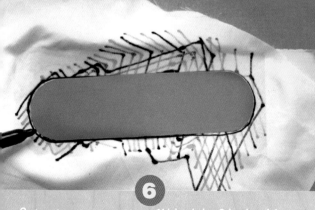

6

Cut out a paper pattern 1½ inch by 6 inch with
rounded corners. Trace the pattern.

If your
bracelet is loose,
roll it up, secure
with a rubber band
and set it in the
sun for a few
hours.

7

Follow the traced line and **carefully**
cut out your cool cuff.

D

ALL

Before modern science and chemistry, dyes were made from plants, insects, seashells, and even animals. Today most dyes are made from chemicals and some are safer to use than others.

Batik dyeing uses a melted wax design that is painted on a fabric and then dyed. The fabric is then ironed between two papers that absorb all the wax, leaving the un-dyed fabric underneath.

100% natural dye made from vegetables is very safe to use and comes in many colors.

Dyeing is the way people have been coloring and decorating fabric and yarn for thousands of years.

There are many unique ways to dye fabric.

ABOUT

You can buy all-purpose dyes in drugstores, supermarkets and craft stores that work well on natural fabrics like cotton, silk and linen, but not wool. When using any kind of dye, be sure to wear latex gloves and eye protection—after that have fun.

There are cold water dyes and very hot water dyes.

Dye can come as a liquid or a powder.

Fabric is made from woven fibers like cotton, wool, silk or synthetics. There is a specific dye for every kind of fiber. Be sure to use the correct dye.

Tie-dye is made when parts of the fabric are tied off with rubber bands or string to prevent the dye color from reaching that part of the fabric. You can use many dye baths and colors. There are many ways to tie-dye fabric to attain excellent and cool results.

DYED PLAID SHEET

This odd dyeing technique creates a windowpane plaid in colors that you pick. Fold your sheet into a perfect square and tie it up just like a present. Dip all four sides in different colored dyes and—ta-da!—you have instant plaid patterns.

YOU WILL NEED
100% cotton sheets in a light color, 4 colors fabric dye, drop cloth, string, 4 aluminum pans, salt

1 Follow the instructions on the dye container and pour 1 inch of each color into separate aluminum pans. Wash, dry, iron flat and fold the sheet into a 12 inch square and tie it up with twine as shown. Carefully dip one side of the folded sheet into the dye pan and wait 5 minutes.

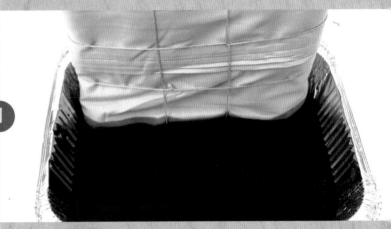

2 Lift the sheet out of the dye and let it drip off back into the dye bath. When it stops dripping, rotate the sheet to the next side and gently place in another color of dye for 5 minutes.

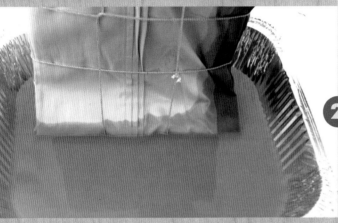

3 Repeat step 2 and change the dye color. Make sure the un-dyed parts of the sheet stay clean and out of the dye.

4 Repeat step 2 again with the last dye color. After there is no more dripping, untie and unfold the sheet, and let it air dry. Then rinse your sheet in warm water and ½ cup of salt to "set" the dye. Machine wash separately on cold.

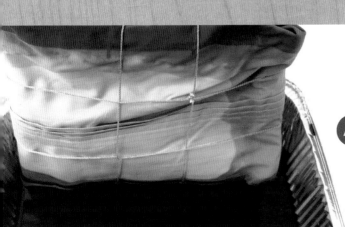

SWEET STREAKS

Dyeing colored streaks in your hair with supplies from the grocery store is super easy and fun.

YOU WILL NEED
Kool-Aid assorted colors (2 packets per color), warm water, hair dryer, hair conditioner, aluminum foil, paint brush, small bowl

1 Wash and dry hair. In a cup add 2 packets of Kool-Aid to ⅛ cup of warm water, and stir until dissolved.

2 Section off the strands you want to dye and place them into a folded piece of foil. Paint on the Kool-Aid dye, making sure to coat all hairs thoroughly. Fold the foil over and bunch it closed to secure the dye inside.

3 While being careful not to burn the scalp, heat the foil using a blow dryer. Let it cool for 20 minutes. Rinse your hair in cold water, apply a hair conditioner, and let it set for 20 minutes. Rinse and style your new colored locks as you like.

SPRINKLED SACK

For a quick and unusual dyeing method, sprinkle dry dye straight from the package and watch the colors swirl and pop!

SUPPLIES

YOU WILL NEED
100% cotton tote bag, 2 colors of dry dye,
plastic dropcloth, water spritzing bottle

1 Wash your tote bag and wring it dry. Lay the damp bag on a plastic drop cloth.

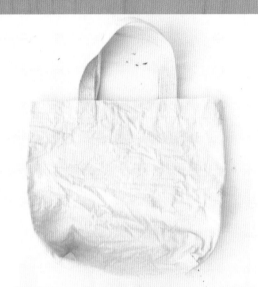

Very carefully snip the corner from one of the dye envelopes and sprinkle the dye grains on the bag in an interesting pattern. Repeat with your next color of dye.

2

3 If you want to diffuse the dye even more, lightly spray water on the bag. The wetter the bag, the fuzzier the design. Let the dye sit for 15 minutes, rinse well and dry.

ICED TEE

Make your own iceberg-dyed T-shirt using a fool-proof technique called dip dyeing.

1

To dip the shirt in the dye, make a support by placing a broom handle on the backs of 2 chairs. Tie the string to the coat hanger hook and hang it over broom handle. Wet the T-shirt until damp and hang on the hanger. Prepare the dye as instructed on the package and pour about 3 inches of dye into the aluminum pan.

2

Carefully lower the hem of the T-shirt 5 inches into the dye bath and secure the string so it won't go in farther. Wait 5 minutes.

3

Lower the T-shirt another 5 inches into the dye and wait 4 minutes.

4

Lower the T-shirt into the dye just to the underside of the sleeve and wait 3 minutes. Carefully hoist the T-shirt out of the dye and let it drip off into the dye. Rinse the dyed parts out well, while keeping the un-dyed part of the T-shirt out of the water, follow the dye-setting instructions on the dye package and wash separately.

SUPPLIES

YOU WILL NEED
prewashed 100% cotton T-shirt, fabric dye, aluminum pan, broom, 2 chairs, clothes hanger, 6 foot string, drop cloth, timer

Italian
Gio Ponti
was an
architect
of great note.
He designed
buildings, rugs
and tiles, even
the inside of
a boat.
With his
clear vibrant
colors and
geometric
forms,
He made bright
modern rooms,
sunny and
warm.

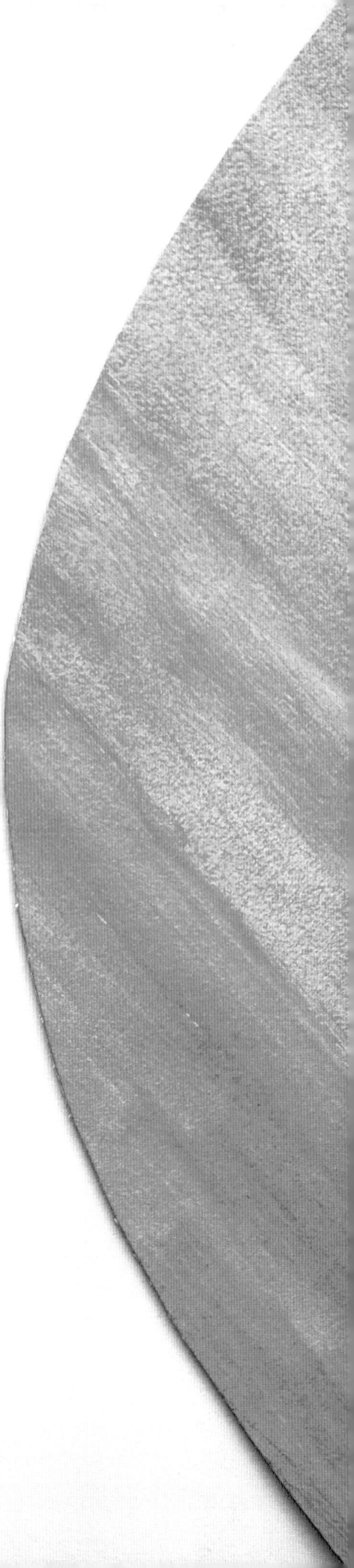

GREAT CRATE STOOL

Here's a soft seating solution for you and your friends! Make a padded cover for plastic crates and a coordinating pet bed painted in the sunny colors of Gio Ponti's geometric tile designs.

PRiSMATic PET PAD

60

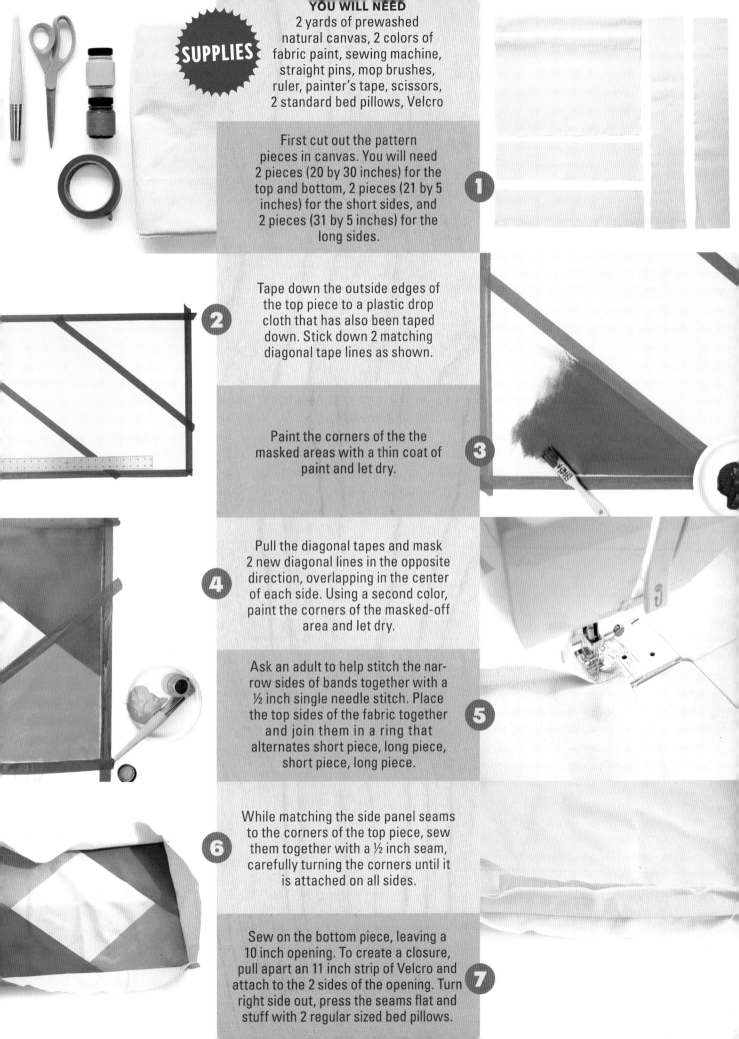

SUPPLIES

1 First cut out the pattern pieces in canvas. You will need 2 pieces (20 by 30 inches) for the top and bottom, 2 pieces (21 by 5 inches) for the short sides, and 2 pieces (31 by 5 inches) for the long sides.

2 Tape down the outside edges of the top piece to a plastic drop cloth that has also been taped down. Stick down 2 matching diagonal tape lines as shown.

3 Paint the corners of the the masked areas with a thin coat of paint and let dry.

4 Pull the diagonal tapes and mask 2 new diagonal lines in the opposite direction, overlapping in the center of each side. Using a second color, paint the corners of the masked-off area and let dry.

5 Ask an adult to help stitch the narrow sides of bands together with a ½ inch single needle stitch. Place the top sides of the fabric together and join them in a ring that alternates short piece, long piece, short piece, long piece.

6 While matching the side panel seams to the corners of the top piece, sew them together with a ½ inch seam, carefully turning the corners until it is attached on all sides.

7 Sew on the bottom piece, leaving a 10 inch opening. To create a closure, pull apart an 11 inch strip of Velcro and attach to the 2 sides of the opening. Turn right side out, press the seams flat and stuff with 2 regular sized bed pillows.

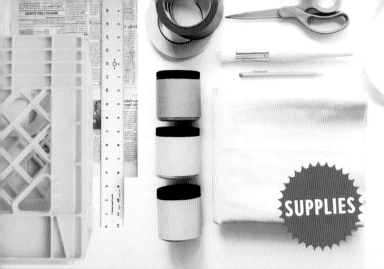

paper plates, scissors, painter's tape, masking tape (for painting stencil), 3 colors of textile paint, safety pin, stencil brush,
pencil, newspaper, ruler, plastic square crate, 1½ yards of
prewashed natural canvas, high-density foam

1 To make the top of the slipcover pattern, trace around
the outside edge of the crate onto newspaper.

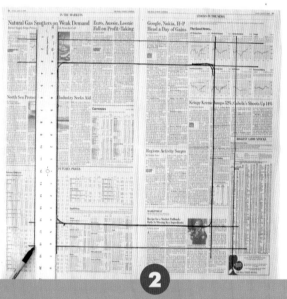

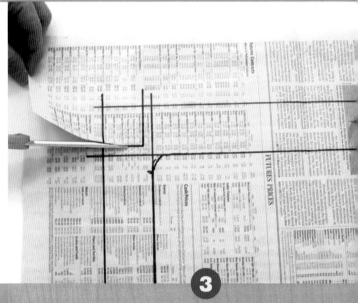

2 Use a ruler to draw a 2½ inch wide
square around your first tracing.

3 Cut out your pattern after you have added ½ inch
into each corner for seam allowance.

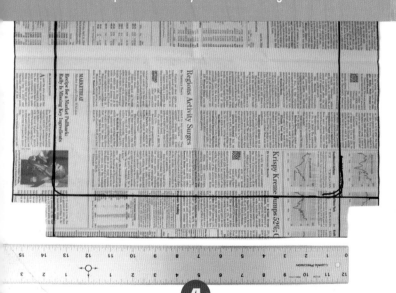

4 To determine the width around the bottom half of the slipcover,
measure around all sides of your first square drawing and add a
1 inch for seam allowance; the height measurement is 13½ inches.

5 Cut out the top piece from the pattern and the
bottom piece from your measurements.

6

nt the stripes on the seat. Use painter's tape and mask diagonal stripes. Alternate painting in the stripes with the 3 colors of paint and let dry. Remove the tape.

7

Paint dots on the bottom part using a masking tape roll as your guide. "Set" both pieces by following the instructions on the paint.

8

size the cushion foam padding, lay the crate bottom on top of the foam and trace around. Cut out.

9

Use a sewing machine to sew 3 of the top piece corners together with a ½ inch seam. Sew the bottom piece to the top, starting at the un-sewn corner, going all around and ending at the other side of the un-sewn corner. Now sew the final side seam shut forming a box shape.

10

e bottom edge up 2 inches and sew through the hem, leaving ening 1 inch wide by the side seam to thread the drawstring ough. Push a safety pin through the end of a shoelace and thread it through and all around the hem casing.

11

Slide the slipcover over the upside-down crate with the foam cushion on the bottom and pull the drawstring tight. Turn the crate stool over and enjoy!

ALL ABOUT

MACHINE STITCHING

Knowing how to sew on a machine is a very useful skill to have. You will be able to hem and alter your own clothes and you can make whatever you want out of cloth. Machine sewing takes practice, so ask an adult to show you the machine basics and sew away!

Edge stitch is a row of single needle machine stitching sewn very close to a seam or edge. This is used for adding finishing edges on shirt cuffs, collars and pockets.

Zigzag stitch moves back and forth forming a zigzag stiching pattern. Use this stitch for appliqué as a decorative edge or when sewing strechy fabrics, so when the fabric is pulled, the thread will not break.

Single Needle stitch is the most basic stitch used in sewing. The lengths of the stitches may be adjusted to accommodate the fabrics that you are sewing.

Roll hem This hemstitch is for clean finishing edges. It is done by folding the fabric up and then folding a ¼ inch of fabric inside the fold and edge stitching along the fold, sewing through all layers.

george

Although a furniture designer by trade,
George Nelson had an eye
for the perfect color.
He made clocks inspired by science,
and home furnishings that
went with one another.

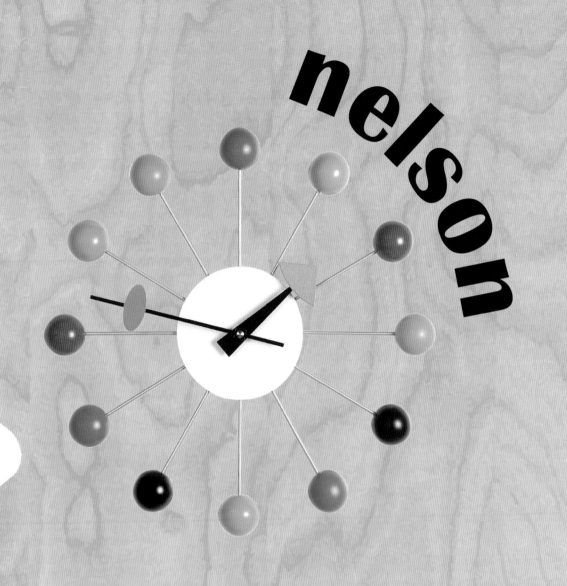

nelson

A sea of white lamps that he once made,
glow in the air like a shiny
school of fish.
He designed a marshmallow inspired sofa,
Rows of soft discs to
sit upon if you wish.

LIGHT BRIGHT

With George Nelson's colored dots as inspiration you can light up your world with this tissue paper collage lamp.

YOU WILL NEED
paper lantern (with lightbulb kit),
many colors of tissue paper, 3 round
objects, pencil, scissors, Mod Podge, paintbrush

1

Using a pencil, trace a circle around a bowl, cup,
plate, or other round object onto layers of multicolored tissue paper.

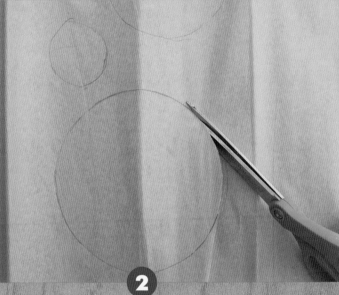

2

Holding the layers of tissue together, cut out
the circle shapes with scissors.

3

Now you have a beautiful assortment of colored dots.

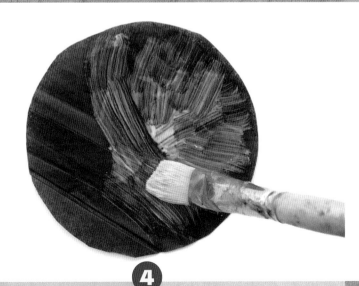

4

Pour a small amount of Mod Podge into a bowl and
apply onto the back of the dots using a brush. Adhere
the tissue dots to the lantern.

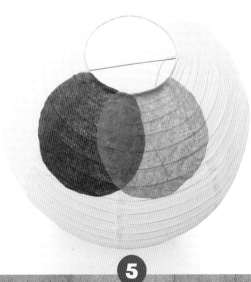

5

Keep applying the dots, wrapping them over the edges
of the lantern where needed. Ask an adult to attach the
light socket and hang where you wish.

SKETCH BOARD

Mixing natural wood with bright colors is a George Nelson classic! Customize a deck in seconds using permanent markers!

YOU WILL NEED
natural wood blank skateboard deck,
many colors of permanent markers

Pick your first color and draw over the
lines of the wood grain until you've
traced the entire line.

1

2

Alternate colors and keep tracing until you
are happy with your design.

Carefully re-attach the trucks and
wheels and away you go!

3

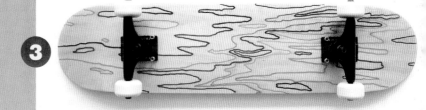

SUPER STAR

George
Nelson
was a design
superstar and
you can be one too.
Inspired by his space
age clock designs,
this felt pillow
will ensure
starry
naps.

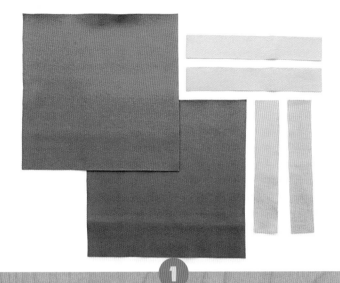

YOU WILL NEED
½ yard each of 3 colors of felt, pillow stuffing, thread, straight pins, fabric scissors, sewing machine

1

From the felt, cut 2 strips of color #1 and 2 strips of color #2, each measuring 1½ inches by 9 inches for the star. Cut 2 pieces of color #3 into a 12 inch square.

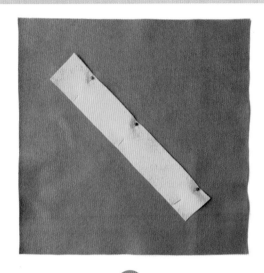

2

Pin down 1 strip of color #1 centered from corner to corner.

3

Zigzag stitch around all sides of the strip with a needle just on the strip's edge.

4

Pin down and sew the other strip of color #1 in the opposite direction and remove pins. Pin down color #2 strips as shown and stitch down. Iron pillow top flat.

5

Line up top and bottom pieces and zigzag around all edges, leaving a 4 inch opening. Fill by pushing the stuffing into the corners. Zigzag shut the opening and press smooth.

Felt is the oldest fabric known to humankind.

Felt is not woven together. It is made by entangling fibers to form a fabric.

ALL ABOUT F

E

Felt is no longer made just from wool. It is available in synthetic versions too.

Felt comes in different thicknesses and is an excellent choice for beginning sewers.

Felt is great for
many arts and crafts
projects because
the edges don't
fray when cut.

Felt is often used
in lots of machine
industries as padding
between metal pieces
or in filters.

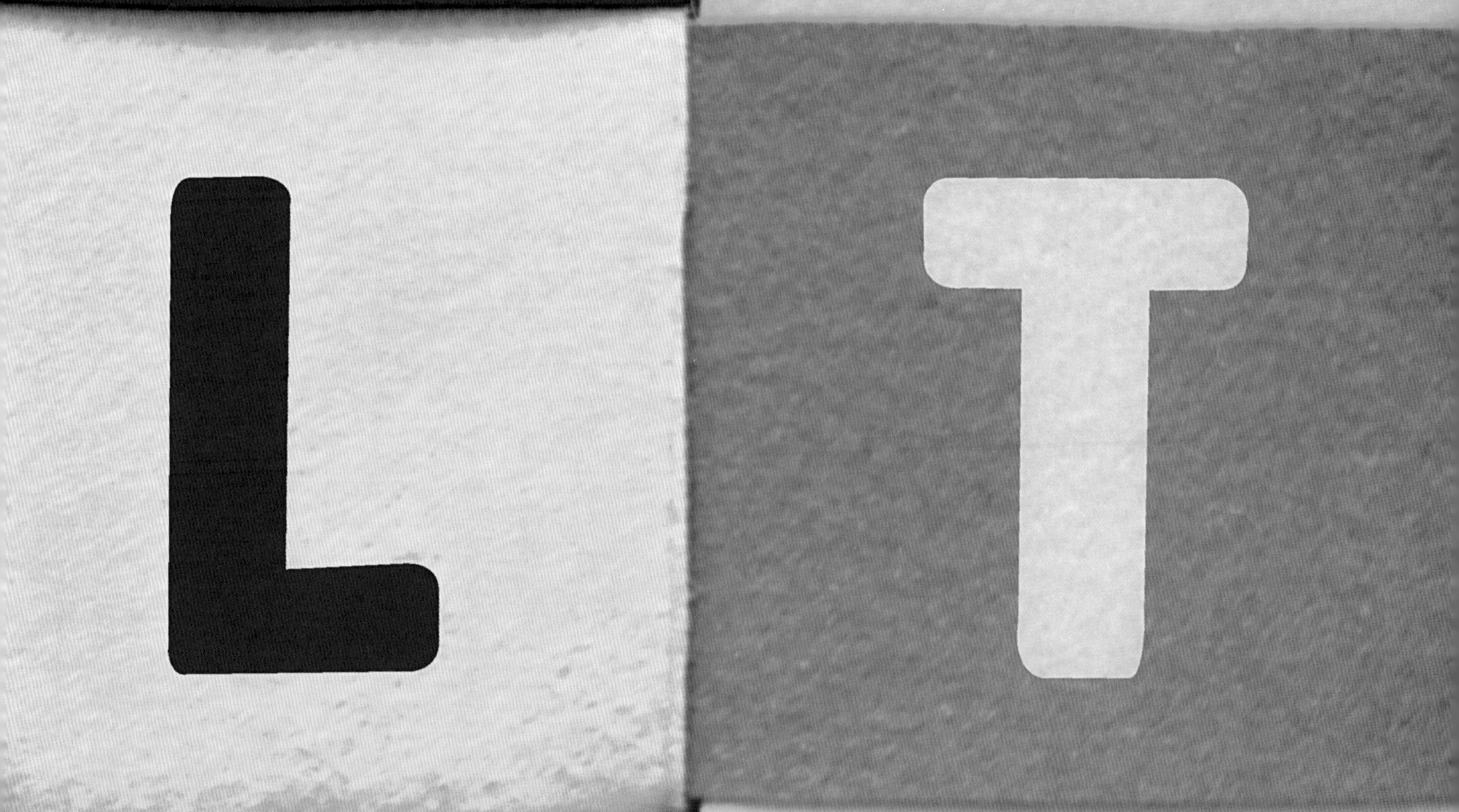

L

T

Felt is great for making
three-dimensional
objects like stuffed
animals or letters.

Felt comes in lots
of very beautiful
colors and is sometimes
embedded with glitter.

MEGA BITE MONSTER

Attack of the mega bites! Make your own custom laptop case monster out of durable felt and fleece.

1

You can download the pattern at kidmademodern.com or make your own.

For the front, cut a rectangle 14½ by 11½ inches from felt color #1. Cut out the eye and mouth pieces from scraps and pin down as shown.

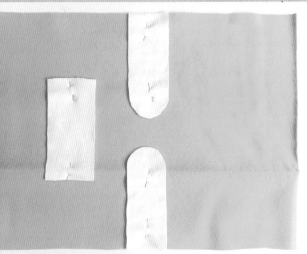

2

Zigzag stitch down around all sides of the trim pieces and remove pins.

3

Cut teeth from another color of scrap and pin down over mouth patch. Single-needle stitch down on straight sides only.

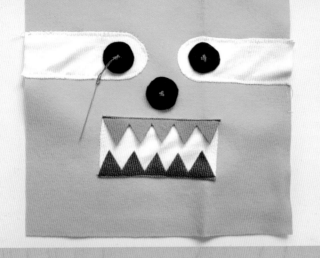

4

For extra thickness, cut out eye and nose dots double layered from scraps and hand stitch on as shown with Xs.

Cut a rectangle 17 ½ by 11 ½ inches from the other color of felt for the back piece. Sew the front and back together with a ½ inch seam.

5

6

Press the seam open and flat. Cut three 18 inch pieces of round elastic and braid together to make a loop 6 inches long. Sew this on at the center top of the back piece as shown.

Line up the edges of both pieces together with the smooth side of the fleece lining touching the decorated side of the felt. Measure 4 inches down on both sides from the top and make a ¼ inch snip through both fabrics. Starting at the snip, sew around all three sides with a ½ inch seam to the other snip as shown. Then sew straight across the other end with a ½ inch seam.

7

4"

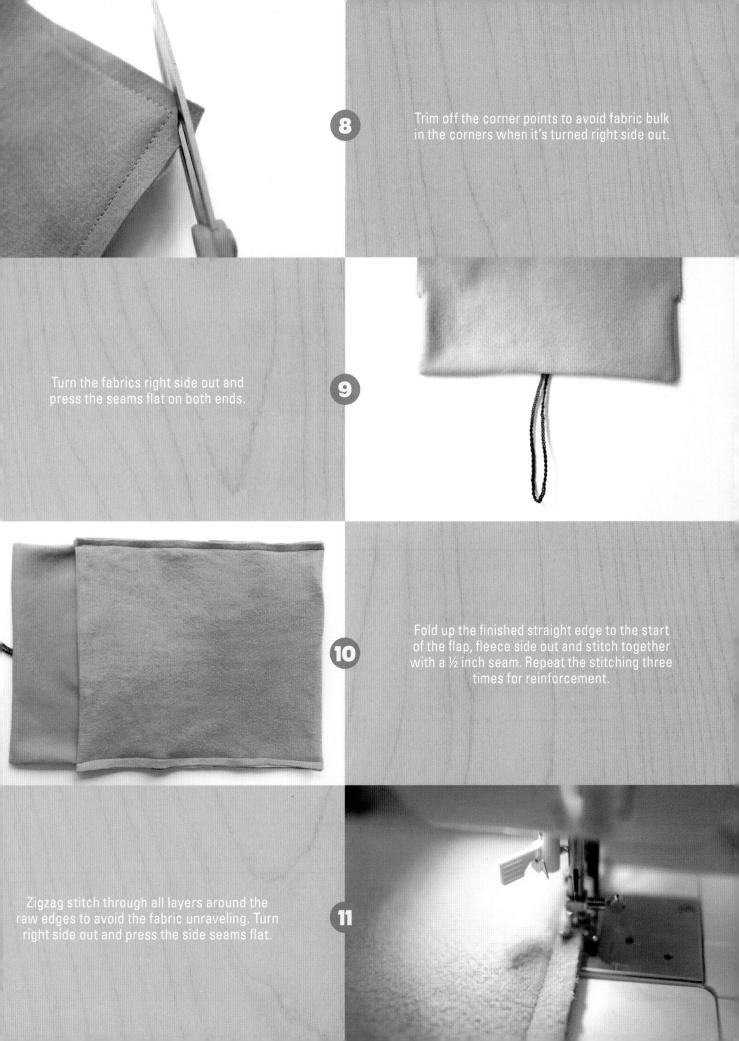

8 Trim off the corner points to avoid fabric bulk in the corners when it's turned right side out.

9 Turn the fabrics right side out and press the seams flat on both ends.

10 Fold up the finished straight edge to the start of the flap, fleece side out and stitch together with a ½ inch seam. Repeat the stitching three times for reinforcement.

11 Zigzag stitch through all layers around the raw edges to avoid the fabric unraveling. Turn right side out and press the side seams flat.

LOG LOUNGE

It's easy to zigzag stitch a wavy wood grained pillow. This log shaped felt pillow slips perfectly under your neck, great for indoor camping.

YOU WILL NEED

felt cut into 2 circles (4½ inches across), 1 rectangle (15 inches by 10 inches), pillow stuffing, sewing machine, thread, hand sewing needle, scissors

You can stitch the wood grain pattern freehand, or download a pattern at kidmademodern.com for inspiration. Draw your pattern lengthwise on the rectangle of felt with tailor's chalk or white crayon that disappears when ironed.

SUPPLIES

1

Zigzag stitch a wood grain pattern that runs across the long sides of the rectangular piece of felt.

2

For the end of the log, stitch a swirl on the circular felt pieces, starting on the outside edge and swirling inward to the center.

3

Place the shorter sides together and sew 4 inches with ½ inch seam allowance from the outside edges, leaving a 3 inch opening that will be used for stuffing.

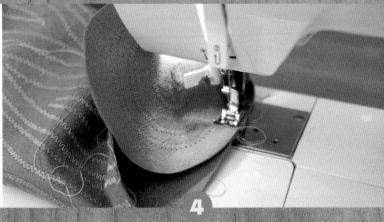

4

Insert the ends of the logs with ½ inch seams carefully lining up the outside edges all the way around.

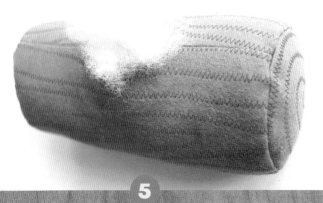

5

Turn the log right side out and insert small bits of stuffing until the pillow is full.

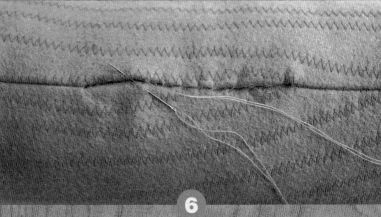

6

With a sewing needle and thread make, small stitches along the seam to close up the pillow.

T TIME

Make your own felt initial pillow with easy blanket-stitch sewing or make a bunch and spell out your whole name!

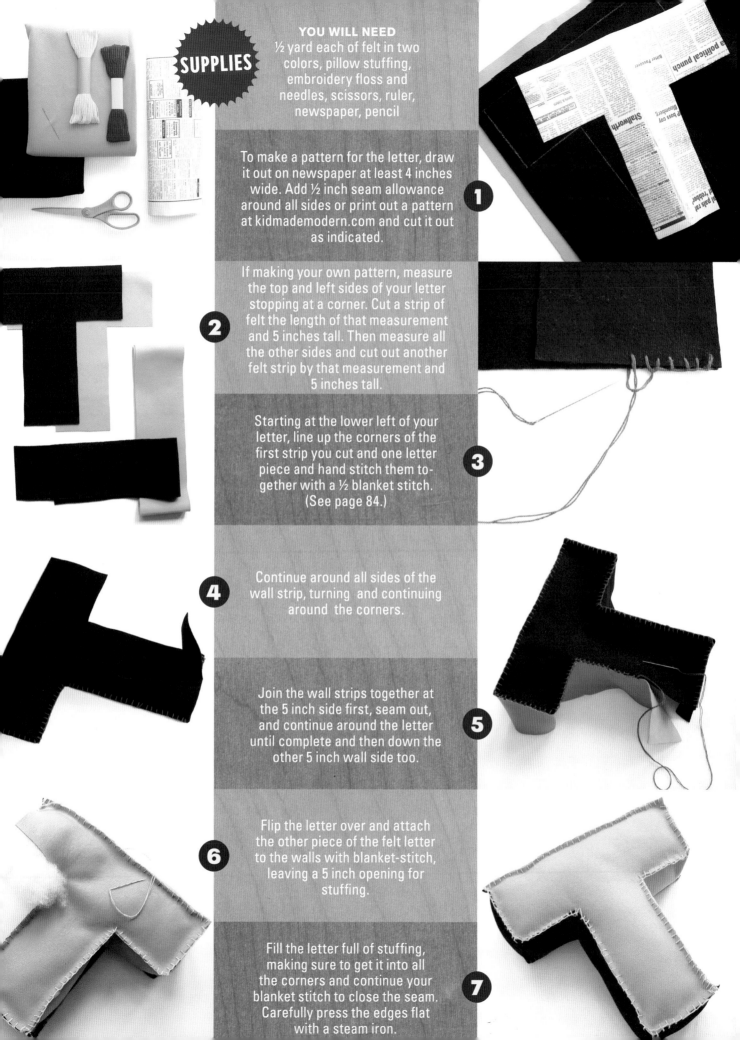

YOU WILL NEED
½ yard each of felt in two colors, pillow stuffing, embroidery floss and needles, scissors, ruler, newspaper, pencil

1 To make a pattern for the letter, draw it out on newspaper at least 4 inches wide. Add ½ inch seam allowance around all sides or print out a pattern at kidmademodern.com and cut it out as indicated.

2 If making your own pattern, measure the top and left sides of your letter stopping at a corner. Cut a strip of felt the length of that measurement and 5 inches tall. Then measure all the other sides and cut out another felt strip by that measurement and 5 inches tall.

3 Starting at the lower left of your letter, line up the corners of the first strip you cut and one letter piece and hand stitch them together with a ½ blanket stitch. (See page 84.)

4 Continue around all sides of the wall strip, turning and continuing around the corners.

5 Join the wall strips together at the 5 inch side first, seam out, and continue around the letter until complete and then down the other 5 inch wall side too.

6 Flip the letter over and attach the other piece of the felt letter to the walls with blanket-stitch, leaving a 5 inch opening for stuffing.

7 Fill the letter full of stuffing, making sure to get it into all the corners and continue your blanket stitch to close the seam. Carefully press the edges flat with a steam iron.

ALL ABOUT
HAND STITCHING

Hand stitching was the very first way clothing was made before sewing machines were invented. It is seldom still used today to construct clothes but is often used in a decorative way called *embroidery*. You can sew these beautiful stitches in a variety of threads, flosses and yarns. Make sure to use the right sized needle for your thread. You can find step-by-step instructions and many more stitches at kidmademodern.com.

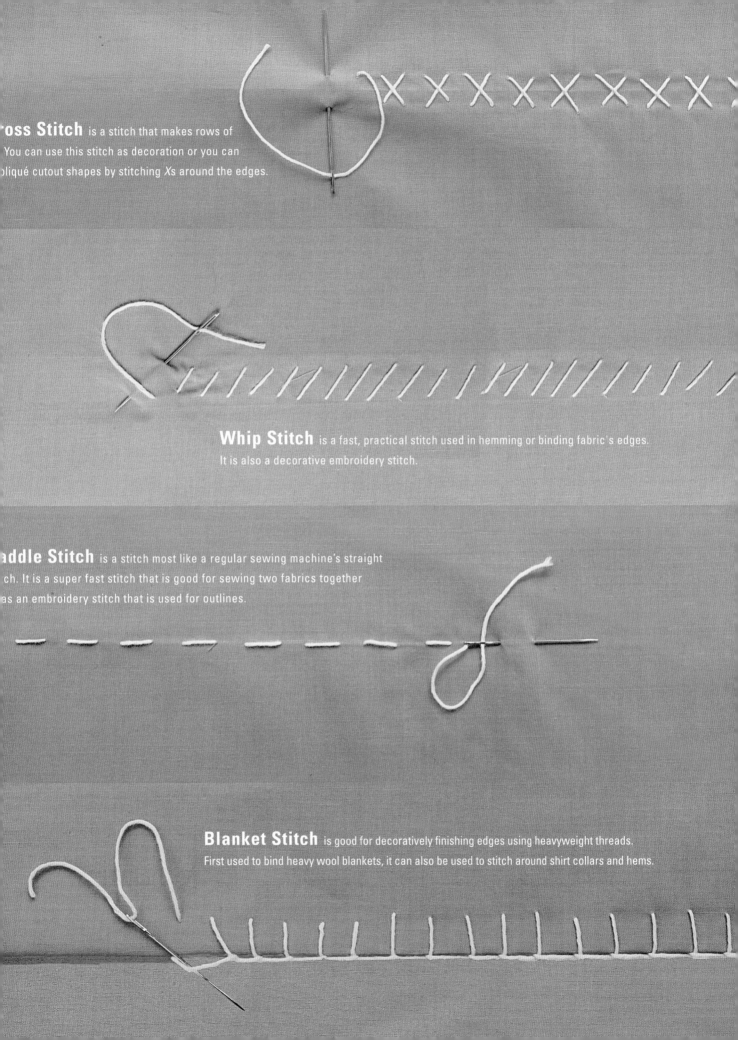

ross Stitch is a stitch that makes rows of
You can use this stitch as decoration or you can
pliqué cutout shapes by stitching *X*s around the edges.

Whip Stitch is a fast, practical stitch used in hemming or binding fabric's edges.
It is also a decorative embroidery stitch.

addle Stitch is a stitch most like a regular sewing machine's straight
ch. It is a super fast stitch that is good for sewing two fabrics together
as an embroidery stitch that is used for outlines.

Blanket Stitch is good for decoratively finishing edges using heavyweight threads.
First used to bind heavy wool blankets, it can also be used to stitch around shirt collars and hems.

Jack Lenor
Larsen is
inventive
indeed,
combining
painting
and poetry
whenever
he weaves.
While mixing
odd materials
like paper,
plastic, and foil,
he turns textiles
into art,
and as fans
we are loyal.

Jack

Lenor
Larsen

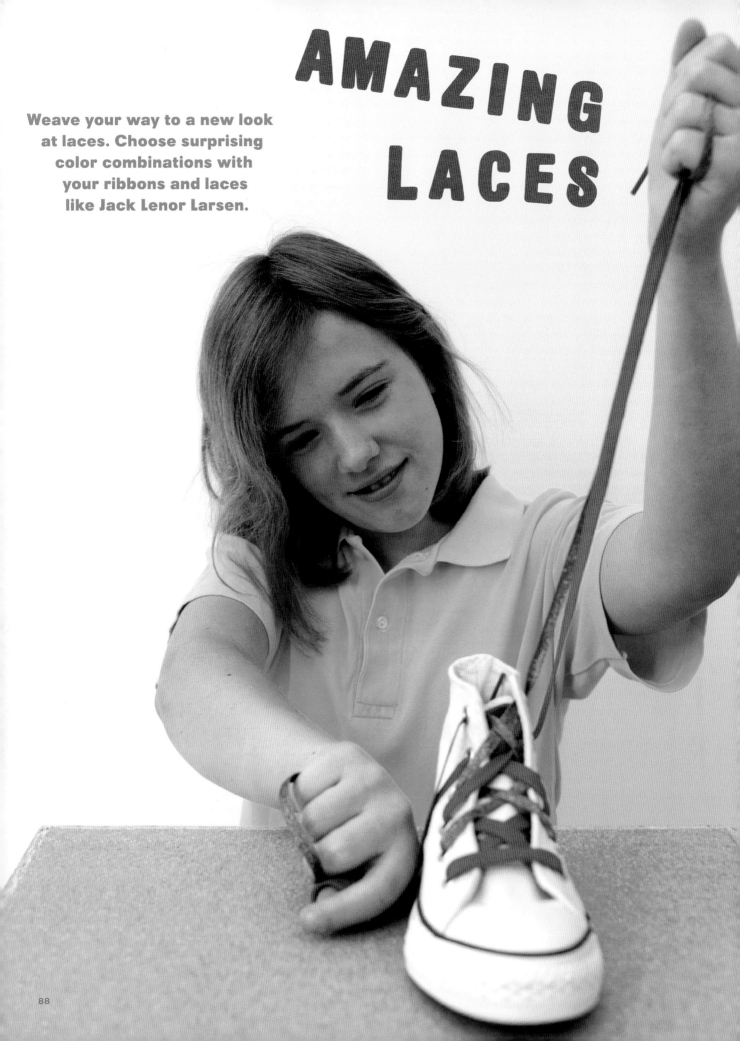

AMAZING LACES

Weave your way to a new look at laces. Choose surprising color combinations with your ribbons and laces like Jack Lenor Larsen.

YOU WILL NEED

sneakers with lots of eye holes, 2 different colors of laces, ribbons, or whatever you want that will fit through the holes.

SUPPLIES

1

2   3

DOUBLE LACE

CHECKER BOARD

1   2

3   4

WAIST WEAVING

All the supplies for this belt are probably in your kitchen right now! Weave strips of plastic bags, old fabric, duct tape and twine together in an unusual combination of materials inspired by Jack Lenor Larsen.

YOU WILL NEED
3 colors of duct tape,
1 strip of fabric 2 inches
wide by your waist
measurements plus 15
inches, 1 plastic bag
cut open and into 2 inch
strips, 1 piece of scrap
wood, two 2 inch long
nails, hammer, two 2 inch
D-rings, twine, push pins

SUPPLIES

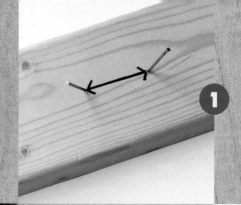

Hammer 2 nails
2 inches apart at
opposing angles
onto a scrap piece
of wood.

1

Wrap the end of the
twine around the
nails and tie a knot.

2

Measure out your
determined length of
three colors of duct
tape and fold in half,
sticky side in. Cut
½-inch strips out of the
folded side of the tape.

3

Insert the 3 tape strips in
an attractive color order
through the twine loop.
Use push pins to secure
materials to the wood.
Alternate duct tape with
fabric and plastic bag in
the center.

4

Weave the long end of the
twine over the tape strips
and under the fabric /
plastic strips, then around
the edge and under the
tape strips and over the
fabric /plastic strips and
repeat, straightening the
twine as you go.

5

When you have woven
down to the end of
your strips, stick a
h piece of duct tape
cross the weaving
d wrap it around to
back. Repeat at the
other end too.

6

Secure the tape
ends and trim off
the rest at the tape
line on both sides
of your strap.

7

8

Lay the strap on the
end of a 6 inch piece
of duct tape and fold
it back onto itself,
sticky sides in.

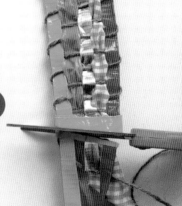

9

Fold the extension in
half around 2 D-rings
and tape down with a
1 inch stripe of tape.
Secure the tape ends
and wear proudly!

COLD

VIDEO GAME

KARATE

METROPOLITAN

computer

A typeface is letters, numbers, and punctuation marks that have been designed to go with one another. Typefaces can help express a range of emotions and add personality to your words. There are two main categories of typefaces: *serif* and *sans-serif*. Serifs are the small feet on the top and bottom of the letters. Sans-serif, which means "without serifs," do not have any flourishes or feet.

ALL ABOUT
TYPE

FUTURE

IT'S SO HOT!!

CHUBBY

DANGER

SPOOKY

Groovy

Elegant

Western

Peace Man

FACES

Serif types are believed to be more legible for reading. Books and newspapers are often printed in serif typeface. Sans-serif typefaces are often used in headlines or when you need to call more attention to your words. Choose a typeface that complements the words you are writing, and it will help express your ideas.

STARS

WOODY

KINNY

GO FAST

ALVIN

lustig

ALVIN LUSTIG IS A GRAPHIC DESIGNER

WE WOULD REALLY LOVE TO SHARE

HE CONVEYED A TON WITH SMALL GESTURES,

PERFECT TYPE, AND GREAT FLAIR.

HE USED WHIMSICAL SHAPES AND COLORS

IN HIS COLLAGES FOR BOOK COVERS,

MEANINGFUL PICTURES OF WHICH

WE HAVE ALWAYS BEEN LOVERS.

BROWN BAG SHOW OFF

the **STAR**

PS139

GYM

SPECIAL GUEST—
ICY
POP

7 PM
25¢

Your next big show deserves an excellent poster! Make your own out of a brown bag in a spare and cool style like Alvin Lustig's.

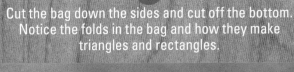

1

Cut the bag down the sides and cut off the bottom. Notice the folds in the bag and how they make triangles and rectangles.

YOU WILL NEED
paper bags, construction paper, acrylic paint, paint brushes, letter stencil, sticker letters, glue stick, painter's tape, marker, scissors

2

Cut construction paper to fit within the folds of the bag. Arrange paper pieces in a checkerboard pattern and glue to the paper bag using a glue stick.

3

Painter's tape together the letter stencils to form the name of your band or event. Use acrylic paint and blot the paint into the stencil letters.

4

Cut other paper shapes like a star and paint stripes and patterns on it, and glue it to the poster once dry.

5

Add your own details using stickers, paint and markers. Now it's time to take your show on the road!

FOLD FAN UP ZINE

This easy-to-make one-page folded zine is a fun way to tell your stories, honor your heroes, and show off your drawings!

YOU WILL NEED

r paper, scissors, bone
der (to sharpen paper
eases), pen, marker,
ayons, construction
paper, photocopier

1

Begin by folding the pages
of your zine. Fold a letter-
sized paper lengthwise
and crease the fold sharply
with a bone folder.

2

Fold paper in half and crease
the fold. Fold again in half as
shown and crease.

3

Open up the paper and set it
down with the paper's center
fold sticking up as shown.

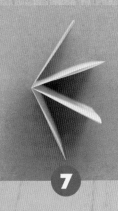

4

en the center fold and
ully make one small cut
the fold in, stopping at
the first crease.

5

Open up the paper and
place it down, center fold
up as shown.

6

Fold the paper horizontally
again. Separate the center
opening by pushing the folds
in opposite directions.

7

Fold all the pages going in
one direction, like a book,
and crease. Now it's time
to design the book.

8

is kind of zine is re-
sible. On one side you
n make your designs
within each single
age as shown or . . .

9

. . . you can make your design
over the entire paper and be
surprised where it ends up when
folded. If you want to make copies of your zine, do it now.

10

To add color to your artwork,
use crayons instead of markers, which can seep through
and ruin your art on the back
side.

11

Refold the paper into your
zine. Making books is
fun, so start on your next
edition!

Tissue paper is a lightweight lofty paper used for many things, including packing. It comes in natural and white and lots of colors that can be used for layered collage.

Vellum paper is an ancient paper once made from animal skins and thankfully is now made from pulp. It is thin and semi-translucent and is used mostly for technical drawings.

Contact paper is a fantastic invention! A plastic roll paper developed to cover kitchens shelves, it is printed with patterns and colors on one side and has a light adhesive on the other. It easily removable great for collages and wall art.

Drawing paper is an art basic that is usually white and opaque. This paper can be used with a variety of drawing tools, including pens, pencils, charcoal, and pastels.

ALL ABOUT
PAPER

Paper has been around for thousands of years in many forms. It is made from different kinds of materials but primarily from pulverized trees and plants called pulp. The gloppy pulp is added to water and pressed into sheets and cut to shape. Paper comes in many thicknesses, opacities, and finishes and can be hand- or machine made.

Handmade Rice paper is made from the rice plant and has a lacy texture. It is semi-transparent and is well suited for collages and lamp shades. You can find it dyed into many colors. Wildflowers and bits of confetti can be pressed into this hand made paper.

Watercolor paper comes in different weights and surface textures, ranging from very toothy to very smooth. This thick paper can come in a tablet form that is sealed on all sides to hold the paper flat and avoids wrinkling while painting with watercolor or gouache paints.

Construction paper is a coarse toothy paper that comes in multicolored sheets. It has a pulpy textured look that shows slight color variations. It is perfect for cutouts, drawing and collage.

Tracing paper is a very transparent kind of vellum paper used by artists and designers for tracing their designs.

Kraft paper is a coarse paper that comes on rolls. Its brown color comes from natural, unbleached wood pulp. Often made into grocery bags, it is best used with charcoals, temperas and chalk.

Cardboard comes in many weights and sizes and is mostly used in making boxes. It is most often brown from the unbleached pulp used to make this double-walled thick paper. It's perfect for building forts, models and masks.

Matte board is a dense thick board covered on one side by a high-grade smooth paper. It can be used for drawing with pencil or inks.

Poster board can be thick and grainy or smooth and shiny. Its sturdy thickness makes it terrific for poster making and gluing things to it, like glitter macaroni!

FORNA

FO

PIERO FORNASETTI made fancy art useful

with simple and modern design.

He always drew his subjects,

using only black and white lines.

SETTI

With the printing press and multiples,
he drew ladies, sunsets and limes,

that are just as beautiful today,
as in the world of his time.

DECOUPAGE DESK SET

Make your very own Fornasetti-inspired furniture with photocopied paper and a special glue called Mod Podge!

YOU WILL NEED
furniture, neon copy paper, scrap magazines, Mod Podge, thick brush, bowl, scissors

1
To prepare your artwork to make black-and-white copies from, lay out your design over the entire page. We cut out barcodes from magazines.

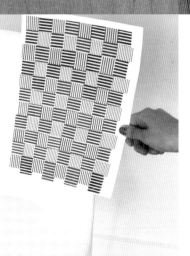

2
Estimate how many pages you will need for your project and photocopy onto colored paper.

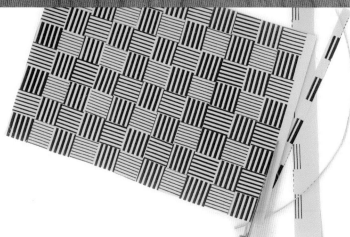

3
Trim out your printed designs.

4
nt a thin coat of Mod Podge over the entire back of the work making sure it is coated evenly. Place the paper, glue side down, onto the surface of your project.

5
Paint a thin layer of Mod Podge on top, carefully smoothing flat any air bubbles or wrinkles. Snip and fold the paper around corners or where needed for a smooth finish.

ISAMU

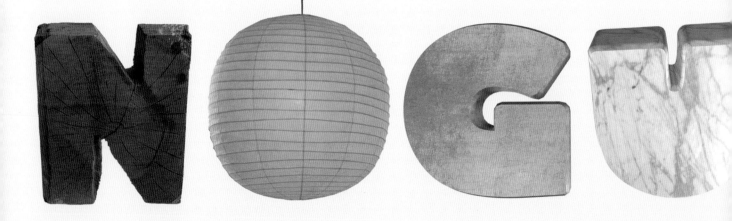
NOGU

He made beautiful curvy sculptures from different stones and metals,
they seem to be reaching upward, inspiring on many levels.
ISAMU NOGUCHI, who hails from Japan,
also made rice paper lamps on a scale that was grand.
Like glowing magic tricks that are floating in the air,
a light show for all, both abstract and rare.

FORM + FUN

This balancing act is a treat to make. Try your own variations of forms and materials to create elegant sculptures like Isamu Noguchi made.

YOU WILL NEED
5 sheets of different colored
poster board, scissors, pencil

1
Download the pattern at kidmademodern.com
or create your own forms from scrap paper first
and then cut out the poster board forms.

2
Cut a slit into the forms as necessary in order
to interlock with other shapes and stand up.

3
Interlock the shapes by inserting them
into and through the cut slits.

4
Stand your sculpture upright and adjust
the shapes until it does not wobble.

5
Attach all other paper pieces and admire
your sculpture from all sides!

LIGHT CUBE

Isamu Noguchi was a master of origami, the Japanese art of paper folding. Fold your own origami paper cubes that glow over twinkle lights.

YOU WILL NEED
roll of white parchment paper, scissors, ruler, small string of white twinkle lights

SUPPLIES

... and repeat on all sides.

6

1 Cut parchment paper into 10 inch squares.

7 Fold the outside points inward as shown.

Fold diagonally corner to corner and crease.

2

Tuck the trangular points at the top and bottom of the diamond into the openings of the side triangles and crease. Repeat on the other 3 points.

8

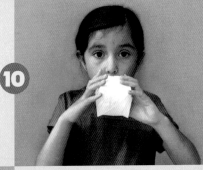

3 Unfold and crease corner to corner again and unfold.

9 Make many lanterns to match the number of lightbulbs.

Id the paper in half nd crease. Gently h the folded corners vn and in forming a triangle shape.

4

Find the hole at the center and blow lightly into it, like blowing up a square balloon!

10

5 Fold the outside points of the triangle upward and crease . . .

Ask an adult to slip the lightbulb into the opening at the center of each lantern and push in until the lantern stays on the cord. For safety, make sure the lightbulb is not touching the lantern directly.

11

CASE STUDY HOUSES

Case Study homes came about when the best architects of their time
all joined together and said, "Everyone deserves good designs."
They made clean lined homes that were easy to assemble and build.
Simple, airy and boxy, they still stylishly thrill.

CASE PLACE

Case study homes inspired this modernist fort made from cardboard boxes and duct tape with simple yet unusual details.

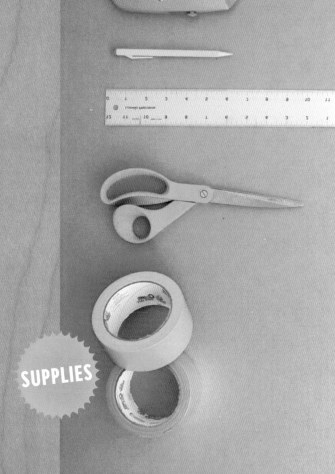

YOU WILL NEED
cardboard boxes, duct tape, scissors, ruler, pencil, box cutter

THIS PROJECT USES SHARP BLADES SO ASK AN ADULT TO MAKE CUTS FOR YOU.

SUPPLIES

Angled Roofs

Mark a diagonal line between the corners of the top flap and ask an adult to help you cut. Then repeat on the opposite flap, making sure that your angles are pointing in same direction. Bend the other two flaps up and on top and tape down.

Corner Doors and Windows

For doors, cut up the corner from the bottom and then cut across the top of the doors on both sides and fold back. For windows, cut a slit in the corner and across the top and bottom of the window and fold back.

Connecting Passageway

To cut your passageways, make an opening that is big enough to fit through while leaving cardboard at the top and on the sides to add to the stability of your fort. Attach the doors between the boxes with tape.

Sliding Shutters

Cut 3 sides of a long rectangle in the side of the box. Bend the cut out in half, slide back your window and finish the edge with tape.

Skylights

You can either cut a skylight into a box or just fold back the top flaps to let the light in. Tape over the edges of your skylight.

LUIS BA

The architect Luis Barragán
had a very vivid style,
his open breezy buildings
made you stay for a while.
Using giant forms, space and light,
in subtle hues and colors bright.
He mixed modern design
with his own Mexican culture,
making some of the world's
most compelling structures.
He uses a whole building
as a painter could,
he put fields of color
where others might use wood.

RRAGÁN

CARD BOARD CASA

Luis Barragán's buildings had ta[ll]
windows and open roofs and th[is]
fort has it all. Try your ow[n]
version using contact pape[r]
to color you[r]
cardboard cas[a]

YOU WILL NEED
cardboard boxes, wood grain and brightly
colored contact paper, packing tape, two tongue
depressors, box cutter, glue, pencil, scissors, ruler

THIS PROJECT USES SHARP BLADES
SO ASK AN ADULT TO MAKE CUTS FOR YOU.

SUPPLIES

Pyramid Shaped Roofs

are easy to do and have skylights too! Measure
5 inches off the corners of top flaps and mark lines to
corners of fold line. Ask an adult to help you cut off
triangle pieces and repeat on all four sides.
Then attach the flaps together with tape.

Awning Doors

Draw a door shape 3 inches in from the top and sides. Cut up the long sides of the door and not across the top. Make a fold across the top and the middle of the door. To keep the door in the open position, tape tongue depressors sticking 2 inches off the door as shown. Make a 2 inch slit in the doorway near the top to slip the sticks into.

Louvered Windows

Tall thin louvered windows are easy to cut. Mark tall rectangles on the side of a box and cut around one tall side and both short sides. Carefully fold along the attached side and decorate as you like.

Cutout Windows

We traced around a CD case to make our three windows. Measure the size you want or trace around something square and carefully cut out your windows.

Decoration

You can use construction paper, tape and contact paper to decorate your modern fort. Cut out shapes that match your windows and doors and attach. Paint can make paper wrinkle up, so it is best to use dry decorations.

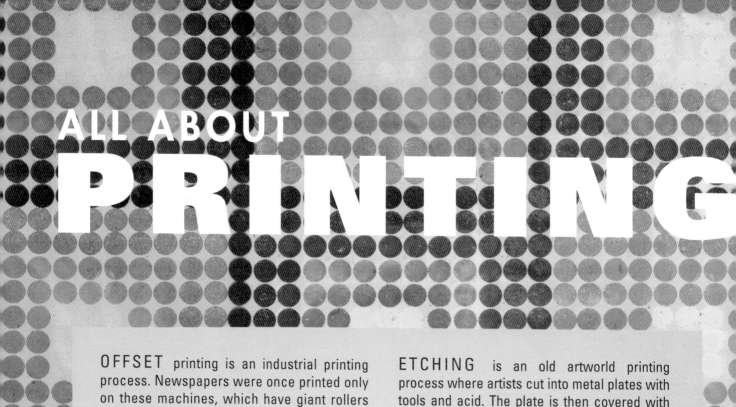

ALL ABOUT PRINTING

OFFSET printing is an industrial printing process. Newspapers were once printed only on these machines, which have giant rollers with images burned in the metal surface, similar to lithography but more automated and used in very large printing runs.

LITHOGRAPHY is a process where the artist first draws on a flat stone surface with oil based pencil or crayon. The surface is then covered with a substance called gum arabic, which sticks to the parts not drawn on. This makes the ink resist sticking where the background is and allows the drawing area to soak up the ink, making the prints looks almost like the drawing itself.

MONOPRINT means only one print. It's made by painting your design, in reverse, on a sheet of Plexiglas or metal and placing a piece of printing paper on top and rolling it flat with a brayer, a kind of rolling pin with a handle. A printer's press, which is a machine that presses the paper firmly onto the plate, is also used or you can use a rolling pin. Pull the paper off, and you will have a mono print.

POTATO printing is a stamping technique where the stamp is carved from a potato, applied with paint and printed on fabric or paper. Scarfed Potatoes, a potato-printing-scarf project is on page 130.

ETCHING is an old artworld printing process where artists cut into metal plates with tools and acid. The plate is then covered with ink then wiped down, leaving ink only inside the engraved image. A piece of water-dampened paper is placed on top of the plate that is run through a high-pressure printing press.

PHOTOCOPIES work by making a simplistic low cost copy of artwork in either black and white or color. You can make artworks and zines with it and can print pages that can be assembled into books. Check out our photocopier projects, Fold Up Fanzine (page 98) and Decoupauge Desk Set (page 104).

BLOCK printing is an old world technique where flat wood blocks are carved with tools, removing the wood away from around the design. Ink or paint is applied to the un-carved areas and printed down on paper.

SILKSCREEN is often used to print on T-shirts. It is a technique that uses a stretched mesh screen with ink pushed through it by a squeegee. A stencil of a design is applied to the screen that stops the ink from passing through. This technique is used to apply designs to fabric, paper, wood, and almost any flat surface.

OFFSET　　ETCHING

LITHOGRAPHY　PHOTOCOPY

MONOPRINT　　BLOCK

POTATO　　SILKSCREEN

Marimekko is not so much a person, but a house of textile design.

With patterns named "big orange poppy," you can tell they were ahead of their time.

They make designs called SUPER GRAPHIC, for them, that's a name that's been coined.

Sometimes their patterns are so gigantic, imagine a flower as big as your home!

BUBBLe WRAP

Marimekko
crazy abo
dots and
are we. Th
painted Bubb
Wrap monopri
makes a brow
bag book cov
delicious
dot

YOU WILL NEED
grocery bags, Bubble Wrap, acrylic paint, wide paint brush, scissors

1

Cut down one side of the brown paper bag and cut out the bottom. Remove the handles if necessary.

2

Lay out your bag flat and cut a piece of big Bubble Wrap the same size.

3

Paint the Bubble Wrap in stripes of your favorite colors.

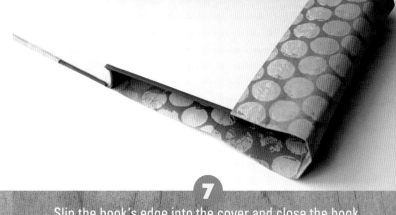

4

While lining up the edges, place the paper bag straight down on top of the painted Bubble Wrap and press down evenly.

5

Pull the paper away from the Bubble Wrap and lay flat to dry.

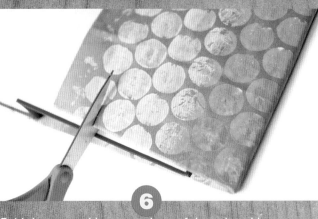

6

Fold the top and bottom edges of the printed bag to match the height of the book. Lay the book on top, fold the ends in and trim off excess.

7

Slip the book's edge into the cover and close the book. Tuck in and adjust the end folds for a perfect fit!

SCARFED POTATOES

It's easy to make a potato printed tube scarf out of a cut-up T-shirt printed with Marimekko inspired geometric patterns.

YOU WILL NEED
XXL shirt, potato, fabric paint, scissors, knife

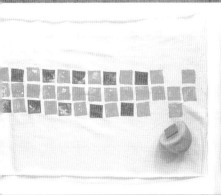

1

Ask an adult to help you make your stamp by cutting the potato in half and then slicing a square form into the cut face. Remove the side pieces away from the square form by slicing inward along the side.

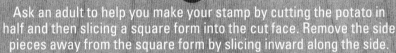

2

Cut across the tee shirt just under the sleeve and cut off the hem. Slide a piece of cardboard or foil inside the shirt to prevent the ink from going through to the other side.

3

Hold the round end of the potato stamp, place your stamp onto the fabric paint, and stamp your pattern on the fabric. To "set" your printed design, follow the fabric paint's instructions.

ROLL OVER POLO

The sea inspired
Marimekko t[o]
make a wav[e]
printed fabr[ic]
and you can to[o]
with this rollin[g]
pin printin[g]
techniqu[e]

YOU WILL NEED
polo shirt, rolling pin, aluminum foil, shoestring, textile paint, small mop brush, painter's tape

Start by covering the rolling pin in aluminum foil. Tape the end of a shoestring to the end of the rolling pin as shown. Wrap the shoestring flat around the pin and tape the end down. Lay the polo down on a flat surface with a piece of foil inside to stop the paint from seeping onto the back.

1

With a mop brush, swab textile paint onto the shoestring until it is very wet with paint but not dripping. Place the rolling pin down on the edge of the shirt.

2

With both hands on the handles, press down firmly and roll across the shirt. Lift the rolling pin off the shirt carefully to avoid smearing. Follow the instructions on the textile paint to "set" your printed pattern.

3

ALEXANDER

Alexander Calder created mobiles,
like giant drawings that move.
He used metal wire to make flat sculpture,
a miniature circus and portraits too!
He made pieces of metal swirl,
like paper in the wind.
With color, form, and balance,
he made sure you looked again.

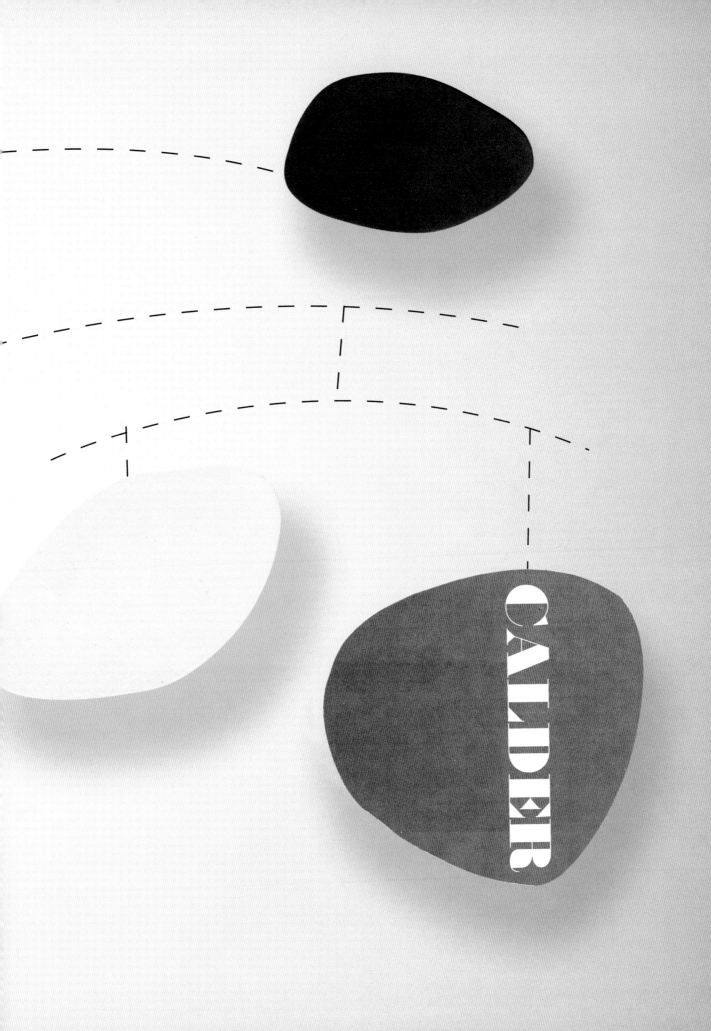

CALDER

MOBILE FOAM

Alexander Calder was the king of mobiles. This center-hung mobile is a breeze to balance.

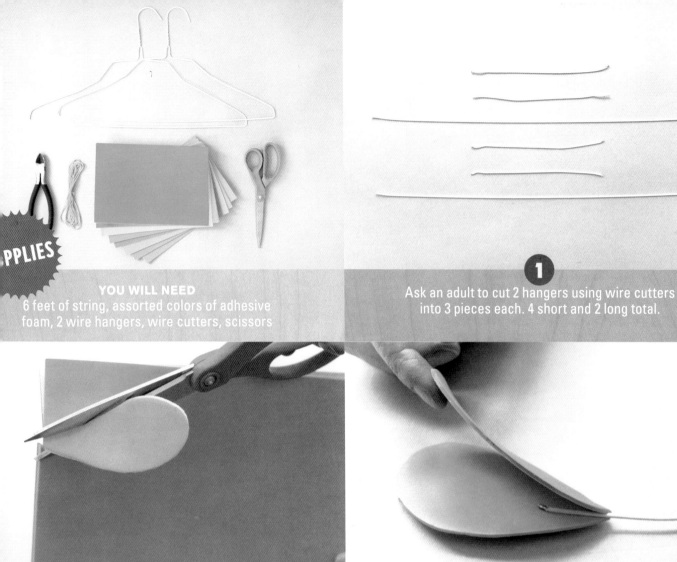

YOU WILL NEED
6 feet of string, assorted colors of adhesive foam, 2 wire hangers, wire cutters, scissors

1
Ask an adult to cut 2 hangers using wire cutters into 3 pieces each. 4 short and 2 long total.

2
ce 2 sheets of adhesive foam back to back. Cut through h layers of foam at the same time, making leaf like oval hapes in various sizes. You'll need a total of 12 pairs.

3
Remove the sticker from the back of the foam piece and lay a wire 1½ inches in. Remove the sticker on the matching piece and stick the two together.

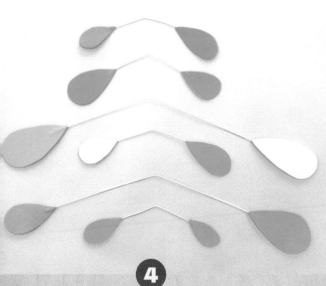

4
Match similiar-sized foam shapes to the ends of each wire. Make a slight bend in the middle of each wire and stack them as shown.

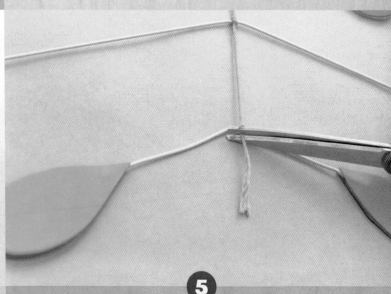

5
Double-knot at the bottom of the wires, bend and trim. Tie knots around the wires every few inches, leaving 4 feet on the end for hanging. Adjust the balance by lightly bending the wires.

WIRED FLOWERS

Wind your way to a beautiful bouquet inspired by the wire sculptures of Alexander Calder.

138

Aster

YOU WILL NEED
Assorted colors of wire, pencil, marker, ruler

Wrap wire around a pencil as shown.

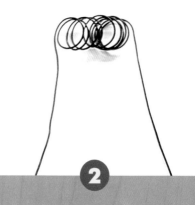

2

Pull out pencil, gently pull open the coil and wrap it around itself to form a flower shape. Twist the ends in the middle of the flower.

3

Wrap a 24 inch length of green wire to cover the petal connection. Twist the remaining wire together into a stem. Gently shape the flower.

Curly Leaf

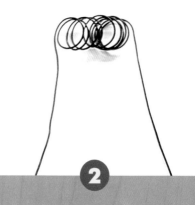

1

Wrap green wire around a marker as shown.

2

Remove the marker and flatten the coil.

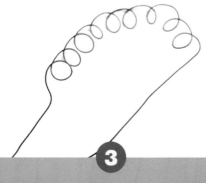

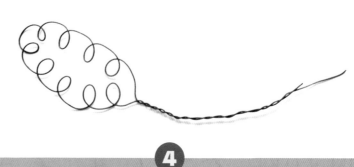

3

Pull the coil out gently.

4

Bend into a leaf shape and twist the wires together for the stem. You can bend the wire with the loops in the outside for a frilly looking leaf.

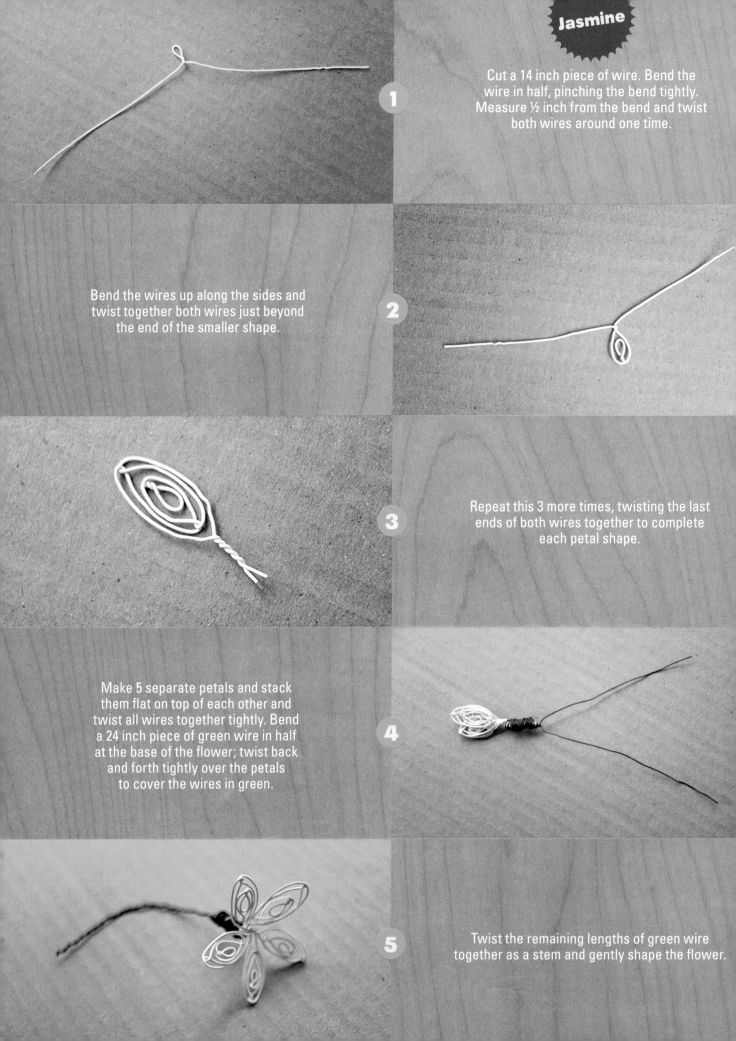

1 Cut a 14 inch piece of wire. Bend the wire in half, pinching the bend tightly. Measure ½ inch from the bend and twist both wires around one time.

2 Bend the wires up along the sides and twist together both wires just beyond the end of the smaller shape.

3 Repeat this 3 more times, twisting the last ends of both wires together to complete each petal shape.

4 Make 5 separate petals and stack them flat on top of each other and twist all wires together tightly. Bend a 24 inch piece of green wire in half at the base of the flower; twist back and forth tightly over the petals to cover the wires in green.

5 Twist the remaining lengths of green wire together as a stem and gently shape the flower.

Mum

1 For the outer petals, twist wire around a ruler as shown.

2 Pull out the ruler and push one end of the wire through the coil to the other side. For the inside of the flower, use a new piece of wire and repeat steps 1 and 2, using a thinner ruler or folded up piece of paper.

3 Pull the wire on the smaller coil through until all the bends form a tight bulb and twist the wires in a stem.

4 Tighten up the larger coil and wrap it around the smaller and twist the wires around the stem.

5 Bend a 24 inch piece of green wire in half at the base of the flower; twist back and forth tightly over the petals to cover the wires in green. Twist the remaining lengths of green wire together as a stem and gently open up the flower.

Mary + Russel

Mary and Russel Wright were
a couple who worked as a team,
they were very smart designers
who rethought how pottery was seen.
They used thick shiny glazes in the
colors of ice creams, picking only
the loveliest shades that make
any table gleam.

CHIP + CLIP

Paint chips and paper clips make up this see-through window screen in a mix of colors inspired by Russel and Mary Wright.

SUPPLIES

YOU WILL NEED
lots of paint chips, paper clips, scrapbook
die punch, scrap of cardboard, push pin

1

Pick your favorite colors and punch out solid
areas using the die punch.

2

Punch 4 holes in the discs as shown.

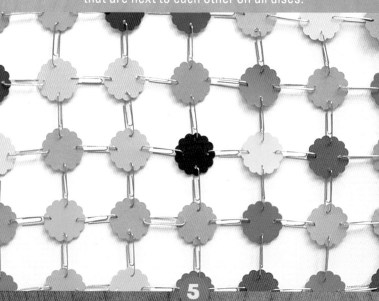

3

Push the outside wire of the paper clip through a hole
and rotate through the hole 2 times. Do this on 2 holes
that are next to each other on all discs.

4

Line up the discs with clips in the color pattern you
wish and begin connecting them together as before.

5

Straighten all the paper clips and hang your screen
with pushpins on your window's frame.

CORK
BOARD
CANVAS

Make your bulletin board pop by painting stripes in the color combinations of Russel and Mary Wright.

YOU WILL NEED
painter's tape,
many colors of acrylic paints,
framed corkboard,
assorted brushes

1 With painter's tape, mask off the frame of the corkboard. Paint a stripe near the outside edge of the corkboard. Paint another color stripe on the opposite side of the board.

2 Continue painting stripes back and forth from the sides until you reach the middle, and let dry. Remove the painter's tape and hang up your corkboard art!

DRAWING is one of the first skills we learn. Knowing all about drawing tools allows you to mix and match materials and techniques as you wish.

Pencils are used for drawing or writing. They are made with a thin stick of graphite enclosed in a long piece of wood, or with a plastic or metal casing. The graphite lead comes in many hardnesses to make different types of marks.

Felt tip pens have a plastic casing with a spongy tip that fills with ink from within. These pens are excellent for line drawings and writing you can later fill in with color.

Oil pastels are like a crayon, only more oily than waxy. They come in dense saturated colors and are great for making painting-like drawings on paper or board.

Pastels are pigment mixed with a binder forming what looks like chalk but comes in many vibrant colors. You will need to "fix" a pastel drawing (which stops the pastels from smearing) by spraying the drawing with a fixative or aerosol works just as well.

Colored pencils are made from pigments pressed into colored leads and made like pencils. Sketch lightly, layering the colors on top of each other for subtle color blending or press down firmly for more opaque marks.

Graphite sticks are molded square pieces of graphite that come in different levels of hardness. This is for drawing on larger paper using the whole stick to make big expansive strokes.

Markers are similar to felt tipped pens but come in larger sizes and more colors. If you leave the pen on the paper too long, it will bleed, making a certain kind of mark that could be exactly what you want. Sometimes markers are smelly and best used in open areas.

Crayons are made from pigment and wax, they are most people's first art supply. They come in many colors and because the wax resists water, they can be used with watercolors for interesting effect. They can be used on fabrics and ironed with a brown paper bag on top to make them permanent.

Charcoal is made from left over burned wood bits, and has a crumbly nature and is messy to use. It can be used in drawing loosely on papers and board.

ALL
ABOUT
DRAWING

Paul Rand

Paul Rand was an artist who chose a path of graphic design,
each time he created, he used vibrant colors and spare lines.

He made thrilling book covers and posters and logos,
and whole books for children that make them go loco!

Paul Rand's book
Sparkle and Spin is a
masterpiece that inspired our
simple self-stick shelf paper mural.

SPARKLE + SPIN

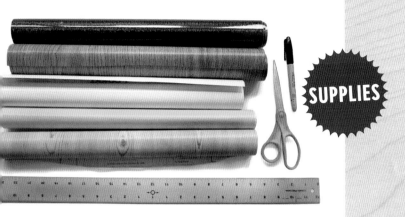

YOU WILL NEED
Assorted rolls of contact paper, ruler,
scissors, marker, plates, small bowl and
drinking glasses for circle patterns,
paper clips

Asterisk
Cut 4 strips of contact paper (2 inches by 12 inches).
Make an + shape, then make an X shape on top.

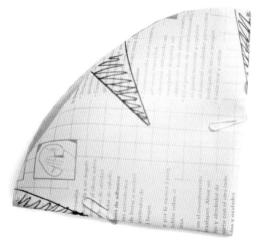

Flower
Cut a circle and fold it in half, back side out, then in
half again and secure with paper clips. Use a marker to
draw 1 wedge shape in the middle and 2 wedges, half
as wide as the middle one, on each side fold.

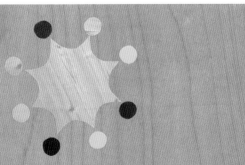

Dotted Star
circle and fold it in half, back side out. Fold it in half again,
then in half again into a skinny pie piece, and secure with
clips. Use a bowl to draw a circle cutout as shown. Trace
ound the bottoms of drinking glasses for outside dots.

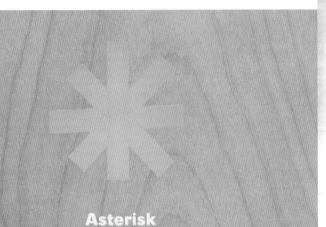

Book design was a specialty of Paul Rand. Design and make your own book with collaged paper and rub-on letters.

HAND MADE BOOK

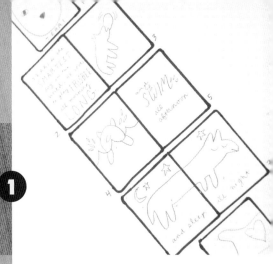

YOU WILL NEED
Construction paper, glue stick, scissors, ink pen, pencil, bone folder, embroidery needle, thread, stencil, sticker letters

1 Make a story board and sketch out your 8 page book. You can download a storyboard template at kidmademodern.com

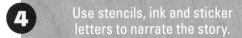

2 Fold a sheet of construction paper in half and cut into 2 pieces and fold them in half. Use a bone folder to smooth the crease.

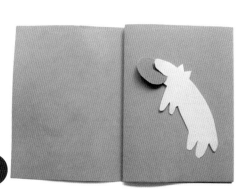

3 Cut and paste construction paper to illustrate graphic images. Use big bold shapes and colors to make clear, eye-catching illustrations.

4 Use stencils, ink and sticker letters to narrate the story.

5 To make a cover, cut a piece of construction paper that fits over the book. You can remove a cut out shape in the cover that shows the first page through it.

6 Open the book to the center spread and punch 2 holes in the crease with the embroidery needle ½ inch from the bottom and top.

7 Sew the book and make a bow in the middle.

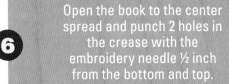

Surprising materials were a trademark of Pau Rand's designs and what could be more surprising than using a potato masher to print a hoodie?

HOODI
MASH
UP

156

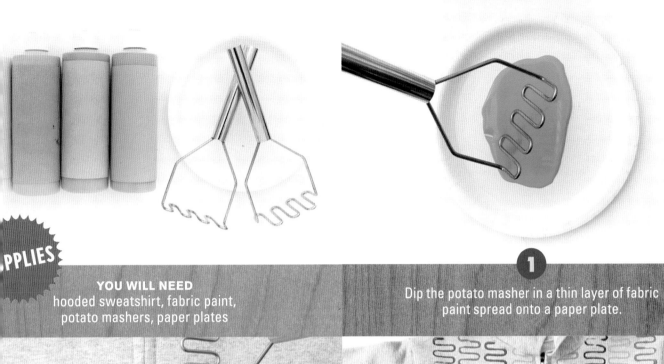

YOU WILL NEED
hooded sweatshirt, fabric paint,
potato mashers, paper plates

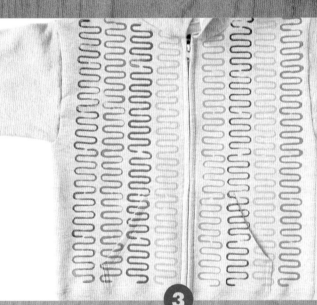

1

Dip the potato masher in a thin layer of fabric
paint spread onto a paper plate.

2

at the center front. Press the masher directly down and
 ay carefully. Re-apply paint on the masher and turn the
 asher to match the lines up from the first printing.

3

Continue printing stripes up the front of the hoodie
being careful not to smudge the wet paint. When dry,
repeat on the back.

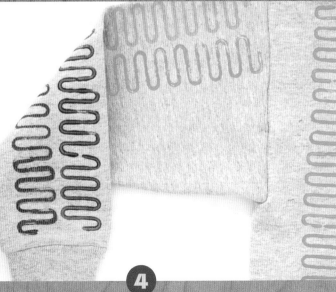

4

On the sleeves, start at the cuff and work your way
up toward the arm hole.

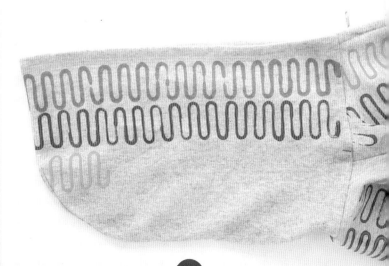

5

Continue printing around the hood, let dry and "set" the
paint as instructed on the paint bottle.

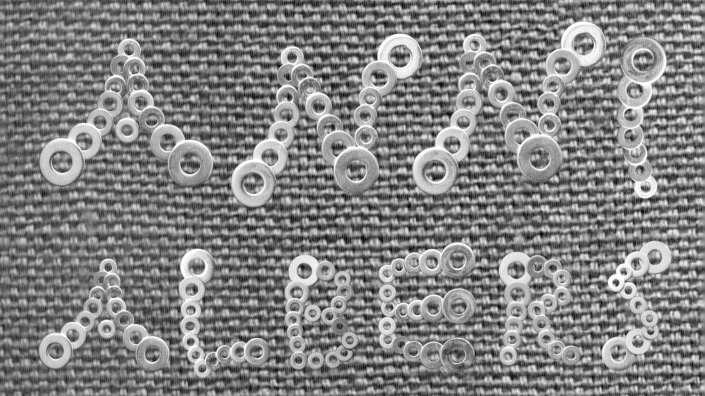

ANNI
ALBERS

Although best known for her weaving,
she inspired a new way to view jewelry too.
Designing with stuff from everyday life,
like washers and strings from a shoe.
The really great IDEA,
that's what Anni Albers gives.
She made a necklace out of sink chain,
and attached it to a sieve!

Anni Albers loved to use everyday materials to create magical jewelry, like this simple bobbi pin necklace.

BOBBI BEADS

YOU WILL NEED
14 bobbi pins in colors or metal tones, one
string of shiny colored Mardi Gras beads

1

Slip bobbi pins in between the beads, starting in
the very middle of the necklace. Make several
necklaces and wear them all at the same time!

GREAT BALLS OF FOIL

Crushed tin foil looks prehistoric and modern at the same time, just like the designs of Anni Albers.

162

SUPPLIES

YOU WILL NEED
bracelet clasp, thick embroidery needle, thread, aluminum foil, spoon

1
Tear a 12 inch piece of foil and loosely squish it into a ball with your fingers and shape by rolling it in your palms. Keep the shiny side of the foil out.

2
Carefully push an embroidery needle through the foil ball.

3
Make the ball smaller and tighter by pushing it in a spoon while being careful not to poke yourself with the needle. Make as many beads as you want.

4
o start stringing, tie the thread to the bracelet clasp. String your beads using the same needle.

5
After you have strung your, beads tie off the end with the other side of the bracelet clasp.

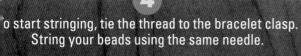

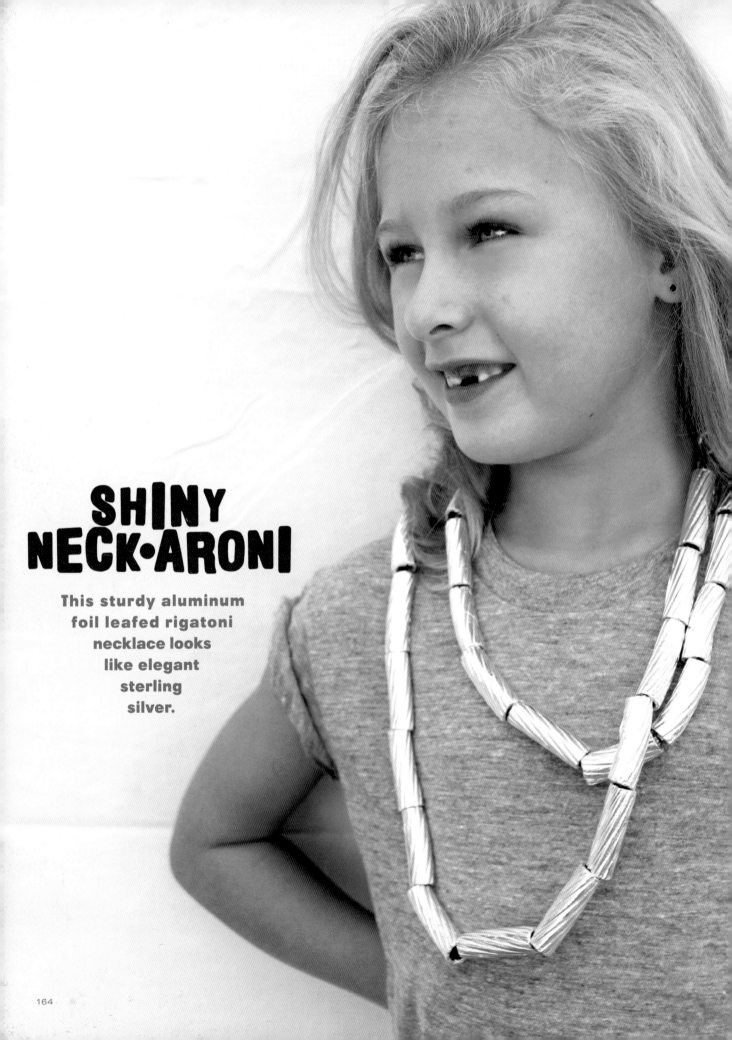

SHINY NECK•ARONI

This sturdy aluminum foil leafed rigatoni necklace looks like elegant sterling silver.

YOU WILL NEED
dry rigatoni, ribbon, aluminum foil,
scissors, pencil

Cut strips of foil that are slightly wider
than the noodle and long enough to
wrap all the way around.

1

2

Wrap the noodle in foil. Using a not-too-
sharp pencil, push the edges of the foil
into the sides of the grooves and wrap it
around the ends.

Make enough foiled noodles to go around
the length of necklace that you want.

3

4

Slide the rigatoni over the string
and tie a knot on the end. Enjoy!

RAY + CHARLES

EAMES

CHARLES & RAY EAMES WERE REALLY QUITE A PAIR THEY MADE ALMOST EVERYTHING FROM FILMS TO CHAIRS.

CHANGING HOW WE THINK WITH ALL
THAT THEY SHARED, THESE KINDS OF
PEOPLE ARE REALLY MOST RARE.

NEVER AFRAID TO
TRY ANYTHING NEW,
THEY BENT WOOD
INTO SHAPES USING
JUST STEAM AND GLUE.

FORT OF CARDS

Build your very own "house of cards"—inspired fort out of decorated cardboard.

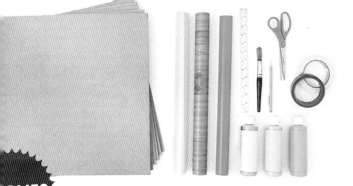

YOU WILL NEED
cardboard pieces cut into 18 inch squares,
ruler, scissors, contact paper, paint, paintbrush

1

Ask an adult to help cut the cardboard squares and
measure 9 inches down on all sides and make a mark.

2

Draw a 1½ inch line from the edge in toward the
middle at the marks.

3

Make a cut on the line and another cut a little bit
over. Remove a sliver of cardboard.

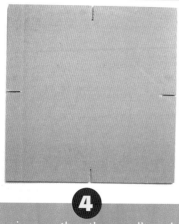

4

Lay these piece on the other cardboard squares
as a template to mark the side cuts.

5

To decorate your giant building cards, you can use
paint, contact paper and markers.

6

Make sure to cut away any decorations
that block the side slits.

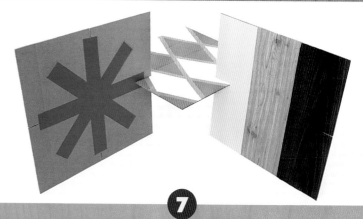

7

Slide the slots of 2 cards together and
repeat until your fort is finished.

PEGBOARD PERCH

The Eames loved to us everyday material like pegboard in thei designs and you ca too with this la desk made from white pegboar and colorfu zip ties

YOU WILL NEED
90 color zip ties, 4 small pieces cut
from an edge of pegboard (8 ½ by
16 inches), 1 large piece cut from an
edge of pegboard (16 by 24 inches).
Cut directly in between the holes and
make sure all the holes line up on all
the cut pieces.

1

To make the V-shaped legs, take 2 of the small pieces of
pegboard and put them back to back, lining up the holes.
Zip ties work by threading the strap end through the eye
hole in one direction. Practice connecting a few first.
Thread a zip tie through the first outside set of holes on
both long sides and loosely tighten the zip tie closed. You
will tighten it completely as a last step. Repeat on the
other two pieces.

2

Attach the legs to the top by loosely closing zip ties through the outside edge holes of both pieces. On the inside of the leg, thread a zip tie
through the top outside hole inward and up through the top piece in the
fourth hole from the outside edge. Now thread back down into the fifth
hole and fasten the zip tie loosely. Repeat on the other side. Now pull all
the zip ties tight, lining the board edges as shown. Finish attaching the zip
ties down the outside edges and carefully trim off the ends. Ask an adult
to lightly run a lighter flame along the cut ends to soften any sharp edges.

KALEIDOSCOPE MOVIE

Charles and Ray Eames made many wonderful films, including one about kaleidoscopes. You can make your own kaleidoscopic masterpiece using a film technique called stop motion animation.

YOU WILL NEED
truction paper, contact paper, glue stick, rubber bands,
camera, two 12 by 14 inch mirrors, tape, marker, popsicle
k, books, ribbon, cookie sheet, video editing software

1 Glue several pieces of construction paper
together to make a long banner.

2 Decorate your banner as you like with colored paper,
contact paper, tape, markers, or whatever you wish.

3 Make ½ inch marks down one side of the banner.

4 Tape the mirror together on the shorter sides.

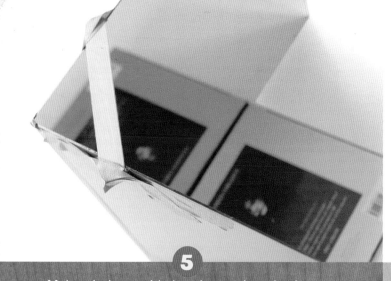

5

Make a L shape with the mirror, using a book as a corner guide and tape the popsicle stick across the corner to use as a handle.

6

Make a stack of books about 6 inches tall, and tie them up with ribbon. Place 2 rubber bands around them as shown.

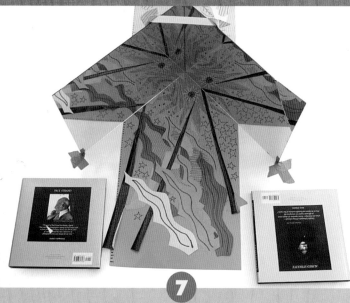

7

Now arrange your workspace. Tape down the front edges of the mirror as shown. Place 2 stacks of books 2 inches tall on either side of your banner.

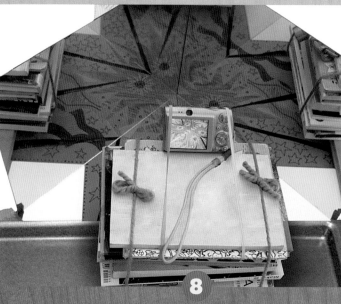

8

Set the cookie sheet like a bridge across the 2 short stacks of books and set the tall stack of books on the cookie sheet. Slip the camera under the rubber bands

9

With the rubber bands holding the camera in a fixed position, aim the center of the viewfinder at the corner where the mirror and banner meet.

10

Making sure never to move the camera, take a picture, th up the stick handle on the mirror and nudge the banner fo to the mark. Repeat until you've taken a shot at every n

Load your images into a movie-editing program in the order you shot them, and make a slideshow using 25 frames per second. Now you are an animator!

WONDER WHEEL

Everything
the Eames made
was stylish and functional,
just like this easy storage wheel.

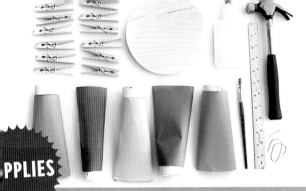

YOU WILL NEED
8 inch wooden disc ¾ inch thick, 12 wooden clothes pins, wood glue, acrylic paint, paintbrush, ruler, hammer, wire, nail

1

Trace the disc on a piece of paper and cut out.

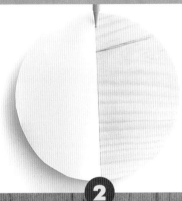

2

Fold the paper into a half moon. Align the edges and make a pencil line along the fold.

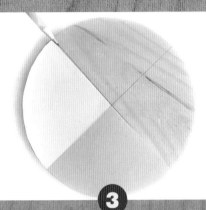

3

Fold half moon paper in half again into a pie shape. Align fold along the pencil line to establish equal quarters and make a pencil mark along the fold.

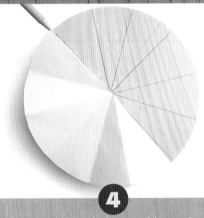

4

Fold paper in half again into a skinny pie piece and trace along folds until 12 marks are made.

5

Run wood glue along one side of a clothespin and center it on top of the pencil lines on the disc aligning the spring groove with the discs edge. Wipe off excess glue with a Q-tip.

6

Paint the disc's center and the top of the clothespins.

7

Carefully hammer a tack behind one of the clothes-pins and twist a wire around the tack to create a hanging loop.

ALL ABOUT CREATIVE ARTS

WRITERS
Writers are like painters but with words. There are many ways to express an idea, and this is how writers make their words special and personal. Writers are used in lots of fields, from the scriptwriters of film and TV shows to authoring novels or even instruction manuals.

FINE ARTS
Unusual and skilled artists can often succeed in the fine art world. Special skills and a singular point of view are very helpful in finding your way. There are many art schools and books available to learn your skills.

SCIENCE & MATH
While not often considered first when thinking of creative fields, science and math are fueled by creativity. All advances in medicines and technology have come from creative scientists and designers.

FILM & TELEVISION
There are many kinds of creative jobs in these industries, such as directors, costume designers, film editors, lighting designers, camera operators, and cooks. Creativity is also needed in executive behind-the-scenes jobs like producers and marketers.

ARCHITECTURE
An architect designs buildings and structures. Special schooling is necessary to learn how to build safe, strong buildings in interesting and new ways.

INTERIOR DESIGN
All the choices in a room's decorations and furniture are made by an interior designer. Interior designers can make beautiful environments for people to enjoy themselves in.

Musicians are like painters but with sounds. There are many musical instruments and ways to make sounds. Musicians can play by themselves or with others in a band.

COMICS & ANIMATION

Comics are a blend between drawings and writing. The ability to show imagery with a story makes very exciting books. Drawings that move are called animation.

FASHION DESIGN

We would have nothing to wear without fashion designers. There are many different kinds of fashion designers, from the kind that make very fancy handmade clothes called couturiers to those that design useful everyday industrial uniforms and everything in between. To be a good fashion designer, it is important to learn all you can about your craft. The best ones know sewing, pattern making, fashion history and all about fabrics too. You can learn about this in fashion colleges or read about it in books, but the best way is to just start!

GRAPHIC DESIGN

Graphic design is a field that has connections to many other creative arts. Film, music, fashion, and writing all require graphic design. There are graphic design schools and fantastic design heroes like Paul Rand and Alvin Lustig to learn from.

PRODUCT DESIGN

A product designer designs most everything we use and enjoy in our life. Whether it's the chair you are sitting or the vacuum cleaner, every bend, knob, and color involved are the efforts of a product designer. A good design sense is needed for designing products as well as an understanding of how to make it perfectly usable, sturdy, and safe.

CREATIVITY is the fuel of life and the basis for success in all the creative arts. There are many possibilities within each of these fields, but it is the mixing of them that makes the most interesting designers. How about being a fashion designer who has the approach of a graphic designer? Or an architect who writes books? Or better yet, a new kind of designer the world has never seen before?

WORD WEAVER

Make sure to save all of your good ideas in this woven paint chip—covered notebook.

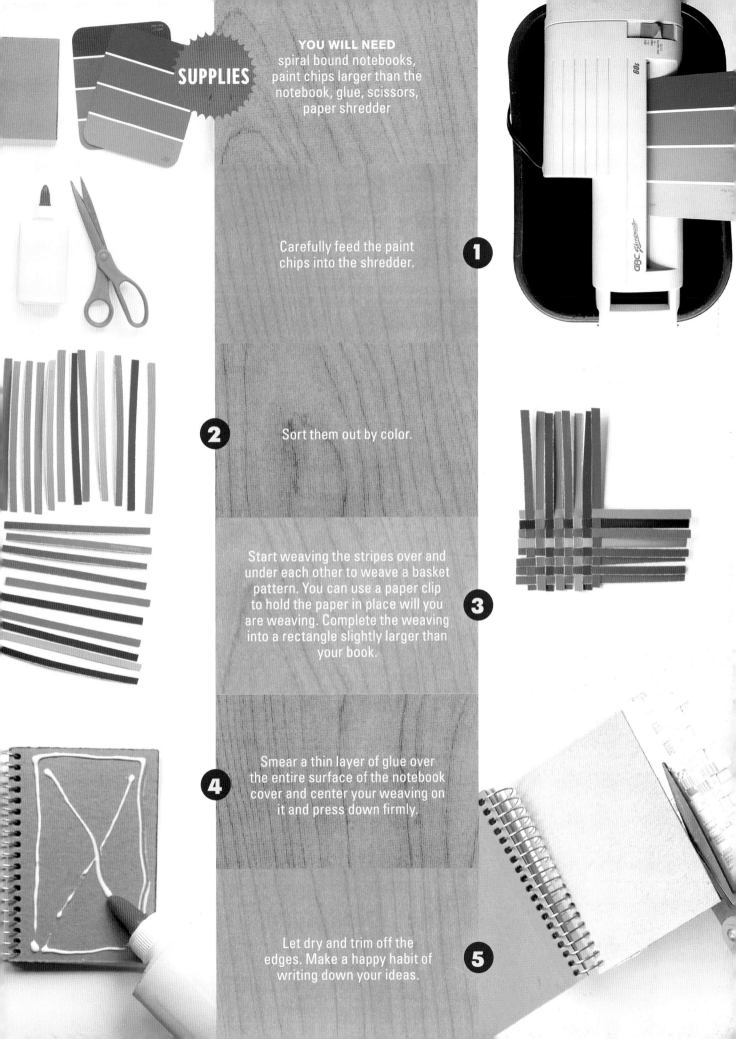

SUPPLIES

YOU WILL NEED
spiral bound notebooks, paint chips larger than the notebook, glue, scissors, paper shredder

1 Carefully feed the paint chips into the shredder.

2 Sort them out by color.

3 Start weaving the stripes over and under each other to weave a basket pattern. You can use a paper clip to hold the paper in place will you are weaving. Complete the weaving into a rectangle slightly larger than your book.

4 Smear a thin layer of glue over the entire surface of the notebook cover and center your weaving on it and press down firmly.

5 Let dry and trim off the edges. Make a happy habit of writing down your ideas.

INSPIRATION SAVER

Organize your inspirations in custom decorated binders for easy reference.

SUPPLIES

YOU WILL NEED 3-ring binder with plastic sleeved covers, scissors, glue stick, 3-ring plastic sleeves, your inspiration. 1. Cut background paper the sizes of the cover and spine openings and decorate. 2. Add press-on type. 3. Slide your inspirations loose or taped on paper into the sleeve opening. 4. Make different binders for all your inspirations!

Always be open
to a new way.

Be honest and honorable in
your dealings with others.

**THESE ARE A FEW IDEAS THAT WILL
SERVE YOU WELL IN BUSINESS AND IN LIFE.**

Plan well and
be on time.

Know about the past, but make
ideas that are brand new.

Be a fan, be inspired,
but don't copy.

Be special and singular in
your approach to design.

There can be a very happy relationship between the arts and commerce. Whether you choose a path of big business or making things on your own, there is always the great possibility of success. You don't need loads of money to start your own business; you just need dedication and creativity and with that you can figure out anything. It is also important to have an understanding of the business side of the creative arts. Like any field, the more you know about it, the better you are at it. There are a lot of ways to share your designs with the world. You can share your creations on Web sites like Etsy and eBay, in local stores or giant chains, in theaters or backyards, or at craft fairs and street corners. Or better still, find a way that's new!!

COMMERCE

Plastic storage bins are a perfect way to store supplies. The bins keep your supplies clean and organized and easy to get out and put away.

Make sure all your supplies are closed well so when you are ready to use them again, they will be in good shape. So screw the lids down and close down the caps!

all about

CLEAN

You will have a speedy cleanup if you take time before you start your projects to prepare your workstation. Get your supplies out and tape down a drop cloth or kraft paper to work on if you are doing something messy. Fold up and reuse your plastic drop cloths.

Learning good tidy working habits makes for maximum possibility and minimum cleanup!

If you are painting wi very messy paint, you can ma cleaning up your fingernails easy by scraping your nails on a bar of soap, getting a little soap under your nails. It keeps the paint away and washes clean.

Take time to clean your brushes well in the right kind of cleaner and always store them bristle end up. If you want to store a brush to use in the future without cleaning it, you can wrap it in plastic wrap so it won't dry out.

U P

Whenever possible, save your supplies and reuse and recycle. It is good for the planet and your piggy bank too!

DESIGNERS TO LOVE
Anni Albers—albersfoundation.org
Luis Barragán—barragan-foundation.org
Case Study House Program—artsandarchitec
    ture.com/case.houses
Alexander Calder—calder.org
Charles + Ray Eames—eamesoffice.com
Piero Fornasetti—fornasetti.com
Alexander Girard—girard.houseind.com
Jack Lenor Larsen—artsmia.org/larsen
Alvin Lustig—alvinlustig.com
Marimekko—marimekko.fi
George Nelson—georgenelson.org
Isamu Noguchi—noguchi.org
Verner Panton—vernerpanton.com
Paul Rand—paul-rand.com
Mary + Russel Wright—russelwrightcenter.org
Eva Zeisel—evazeisel.com

MORE DESIGNERS TO LOVE
Alvar Aalto—aalto.com
Harry Bertoia—bertoiaharry.com
Marcel Breuer—marcelbreuer.org
Dorothy Draper—dorothydraper.com
Philip Johnson—philipjohnsonglasshouse.org
Arne Jacobsen—arne-jacobsen.com
Vladimir Kagan—vladimirkagan.com
George Nakashima—nakashimawoodworker.com
Oscar Niemeyer—niemeyer.org.br
Jens Risom—risom.org
Eero Saarinen—eerosaarinen.net
Art Smith—brooklynmuseum.org/exhibitions/art_smith
Ilmari Tapiovaara—ilmaritapiovaara.fi

ART + CRAFT STORES
Pearl Fine Art Supplies—pearlpaint.com
New York Central Art Supply—nycentralart.com
Soho Art Materials—sohoartmaterials.com
Dick Blick Art Materials—dickblick.com
Purl—purlsoho.com
Spacecraft Brooklyn—spacecraftbrooklyn.com
Con-Tact Brand—contactbrand.com
Michael's—michaels.com
FeltPro—feltpro.net
Uline—uline.com

BLOGS + WEB SITES
d-i-y-kids.blogspot.com
bkids.typepad.com
ohdeedoh.com
2modern.blogs.com
printpattern.blogspot.com
marthastewart.com/kids
houseind.com/showandtell
ilovetypography.com
kindraishere.blogspot.com
finelittleday.blogspot.com
skout.co.nz
smartsandcrafts.com
designspongeonline.com
belladia.typepad.com/crafty_crow

MUSEUMS TO VISIT

NEW YORK
The Museum of Modern Art—moma.org
Cooper-Hewitt Nat'l Design Museum—cooperhewitt.org
Guggenheim Museum—guggenheim.org
Museum of Arts and Design—madmuseum.org
Museum of Comic and Cartoon—moccany.org
Neue Gallery—neuegalerie.org
Brooklyn Museum—brooklynmuseum.org
New Museum—newmuseum.org
The Drawing Center—drawingcenter.org
The Childrens Museum of Manhattan—cmom.org
American Museum of the Moving Image—movingimage.us
American Folk Art Museum—folkartmuseum.org
Whitney Museum of American Art—whitney.org
Metropolitan Museum of Art—metmuseum.org
Brooklyn Children's Museum—brooklynkids.org

CALIFORNIA
San Francisco Museum of Modern Art—sfmoma.org
Pasadena Museum of California Art—pmcaonline.org
Los Angeles County Museum of Art—lacma.org
J. Paul Getty Museum—getty.edu/museum
Museum of Contemporary Art Los Angeles—moca-la.org
Exploratorium—exploratorium.edu

MASSACHUSETTS
Mass. Museum of Contemporary Art—massmoca.org
Boston Children's Museum—bostonchildrensmuseum.org
The Institute of Contemporary Art—icaboston.org

ILLINOIS
Museum of Contemporary Art—mcachicago.org
The Museum of Science and Industry—msichicago.org

PENNSLYVANIA
The Philadelphia Museum of Art—philamuseum.org
The Fabric Workshop and Museum—fabricworkshop.org

WASHINGTON, DC
Smithsonian Institution—si.edu

MARYLAND
American Visionary Art Museum—avam.org

MINNESOTA
Walker Art Center—walkerart.org

ALABAMA
Rural studio—cadc.auburn.edu/soa/rural-studio

FLORIDA
Wolfsonian—wolfsonian.org

OHIO
Wexner Center for the Arts—wexarts.org

LONDON
Tate : British & Int'l Modern Contempoary Art—tate.org
The Victoria and Albert Museum—vam.ac.uk
Design Museum—designmuseum.org

EUROPE
Louisiana Museum of Modern Art—louisiana.dk/dk
Stedelijk Museum—stedelijkindestad.nl
Vitra Design Museum—design-museum.de
Bauhaus Archive Museum—bauhaus.de/english
Guggenheim Museum—guggenheim.org/bilboa
Museo National Del Prado—museodelprado.es
Centre Pompidou—centrepompidou.fr
Louvre—louvre.fr
Picasso Museum—museupicasso.bcn.es/en

READING LIST

Guide to Easier Living by Mary and Russel Wright
Kids Knitting by Melanie Falick
The Guerilla Art Kit by Keri Smith
Textile Designs: Two Hundred Years of European and American Patterns Organized by Motif, Style, Color, Layout, and Period by Susan Meller and Joost Elffers
Paul Rand by Steven Heller
Lotta Prints by Lotta Jansdotter
Printing by Hand by Lena Corwin
Making Books by Hand: A Step-by-Step Guide by Mary McCarthy and Phillip Manna
How to Make Books: Fold, Cut & Stitch Your Way to a One-of-a-Kind Book by Esther K. Smith
Eva Zeisel on Design by Eva Zeisel
George Nelson: Compact Design Portfolio by Michael Webb
Charley Harper : An Illustrated Life by Todd Oldham
Charley Harper's Bird and Words by Charley Harper
Design Handbook: Concepts, Materials, Styles by Charlotte and Peter Fiell
Design of the 20th Century by Charlot Fiell
The Art of Manipulating Fabric by Colette Wolff
Alexander Girard Designs for Herman Miller by Leslie Pina
Drawing a Tree by Bruno Munari
George Nelson: The Design of Modern Design by Stanley Abercrombie
An Eames Primer by Eames Demetrios
Fornasetti: Designer of Dreams by Patrick Mauries
Marimekko: Fabrics Fashion and Architecture by Ms. Marianne Aav
The Soul of a Tree : A Master Woodworkers Reflections by George Nakashima
Hand Made Nation by Faythe Levine and Courtney Helmerl
ReadyMade: How to Make (Almost) Everything by Shoshana Berger and Grace Hawthorne
Stencil 101 by Ed Roth
Over and Over: A Catalog of Hand-Drawn Patterns by Michael Perry
D.I.Y. Kids by Ellen and Julia Lupton
Wallpaper Projects by Lauren Smith and Derek Fagerstrom
The *Work of Charles and Ray Eames* by Donald Albrecht
Julius Shulman : Architecture and Its Photography by Peter Gössel
Knoll Furniture by Steven and Linda Rouland
Case Study Houses by Elizabeth Smith and Peter Goessel
Modernist Jewelry 1930–1960 by Marbeth Schon

BOOK DEPT
WISHES TO THANK

- -

Steve, Gloria,
Miles + Lola Crist
Paul and Tinti Norton
Reid Embrey

Linda Oldham
Granny Jasper
Jack Oldham
Mikell and Scott Morrow
Brad Oldham
Robin Oldham
Presley Oldham

Jose Abellar
Mimi Pond and Wayne,
Woodrow + Lulu White
Michele Romero
Vital Vayness

Jessica Pigza
Urvi Dalal
Sigrid Keough
Courtney Moore
Carolyn Kelly
Robin Winters
Dorice Alexander

Models:
Paloma Abellar
Samir Dalal
Olivia-Keough
Devin Moore
Rylie Morrow

Silkscreen on pg 125
by Michele Romero
Monoprint on pg 125
by Wayne White
Zine on pg 176
by Noah Lyon

KID MADE MODERN
by Todd Oldham
kidmademodern.com

Copyright ©2012 AMMO Books, LLC

Designed by Book Dept.
Book Dept. is Todd Oldham,
Kelly Rakowski + Matt Cassity
Designer prose by Hillary Moore
Photography by Todd, Kelly, Matt +
Hillary

ISBN: 9781934429884
Library of Congress Number: 2012930847

Printed in China

www.ammobooks.com

KID MADE MODERN MADE BY

TODD OLDHAM

ANN

TONY LONGORIA

JOSH GEURTSEN

KELLY RAKOWSKI

MATT CASSITY

YOSHI FUNATANI

CONN BRATTAIN

HILLARY MOORE

KELLI HARTLINE

JEN NIELSEN

JOHN WEIGOLD

ENJOY!